Vivendi

This book identifies and analyses the main socio-economic trends that characterize Vivendi, the French mass media conglomerate, and explores how they have oriented its development and evolution.

Philippe Bouquillion explores the industrial, financial, globalization and public policy issues in the various sectors in which Vivendi is involved, paying particular attention to recorded music, pay television, publishing, video games, advertising and telecommunications. He examines Vivendi's role as a key global player in the entertainment and cultural industries as a result of its established position as world number one in recorded music via Universal Music Group. He also highlights Vivendi's involvement in various national markets, including their notable strategies in African markets and their significance in the telecommunications and television markets in Italy.

This book will be of interest to students, scholars and researchers of global media, media and cultural industries, and political economy.

Philippe Bouquillion is Professor of Communication at University Paris Sorbonne Nord and a Researcher at the Laboratory of Excellence (Cultural Industries and Artistic Creation). He is the director of the Laboratory of Information and Communication Sciences (LabSIC). His work focuses on cultural and creative industries, particularly the issues of concentration and financialization, transnationalization, and the transformations of public policies. His most recent research deals with audiovisual digital platforms in Europe and India.

Global Media Giants
Series editors: Benjamin J. Birkinbine, Rodrigo Gomez and Janet Wasko

Since the second half of the 20th century, the significance of media corporate power has been increasing in different and complex ways around the world; the power of these companies in political, symbolic and economic terms has been a global issue and concern. In the 21st century, understanding media corporations is essential to understanding the political, economic and socio-cultural dimensions of our contemporary societies.

The **Global Media Giants** series continues the work that began in the series editors' book *Global Media Giants*, providing detailed examinations of the largest and most powerful media corporations in the world.

Grupo Prisa
Media Power in Contemporary Spain
Luis A. Albornoz, Ana I. Segovia, and Núria Almiron

Amazon
Understanding a Global Communication Giant
Benedetta Brevini and Lukasz Swiatek

Grupo Clarín
From Argentine Newspaper to Convergent Media Conglomerate
Guillermo Mastrini, Martín Becerra, and Ana Bizberge

Vivendi
A Key Player in Global Entertainment and Media
Philippe Bouquillion

For more information about this series, please visit: https://www.routledge.com/Global-Media-Giants/book-series/GMG

Vivendi
A Key Player in Global Entertainment and Media

Philippe Bouquillion

NEW YORK AND LONDON

First published 2021
by Routledge
605 Third Avenue, New York, NY 10158

and by Routledge
2 Park Square, Milton Park, Abingdon, Oxon, OX14 4RN

Routledge is an imprint of the Taylor & Francis Group, an informa business

© 2021 Philippe Bouquillion

The right of Philippe Bouquillion to be identified as author of this work has been asserted by him in accordance with sections 77 and 78 of the Copyright, Designs and Patents Act 1988.

All rights reserved. No part of this book may be reprinted or reproduced or utilised in any form or by any electronic, mechanical, or other means, now known or hereafter invented, including photocopying and recording, or in any information storage or retrieval system, without permission in writing from the publishers.

Trademark notice: Product or corporate names may be trademarks or registered trademarks, and are used only for identification and explanation without intent to infringe.

Library of Congress Cataloging-in-Publication Data
A catalog record for this title has been requested

ISBN: 978-0-367-55782-9 (hbk)
ISBN: 978-0-367-55783-6 (pbk)
ISBN: 978-1-003-09511-8 (ebk)

Typeset in Times New Roman
by codeMantra

Contents

Acknowledgments ix

1 **Introduction** 1
  Methods and Sources 6

2 **Vivendi's History and Context** 8
  The "ancestors" 8
  From the CGE to Vivendi: The Emergence of a Powerful Private Industrial Player in French Media and Culture in the 1980s 10
  From Vivendi to Vivendi Universal 12
  Back to Vivendi: The Company Came Close to Bankruptcy but Multiplied Sales and Acquisitions 17
  Vivendi: A Player in the Media Sector or Various Assets for Sale? 21

3 **Vivendi's Economic Profile** 27
  Under the Leadership of Vincent Bolloré and His Group, Vivendi Is Experiencing a Strong Expansion Phase 28
    Vivendi Acquires Audiovisual Assets 28
    Vivendi Regains Control of Havas 31
    Vivendi Regains a Foothold in Video Games 31
    Vivendi Relaunches Its Book Publishing Activities 32

The Company Again Acquires Assets in
  Telecommunications 33
A Very Profitable Trip to the Capital of the FNAC
  Group 35
A Partial Sale of the Capital of Universal
  Music Group 35
The Takeover Bid for Lagardère 36
What Can We Conclude from the Outcome of
  All These Operations? 39
*Vivendi, a Conglomerate of Business Activities with
  Few Synergies and Very Different Dynamics 40*
Universal Music Group 45
The Canal+ Group 47
The Havas Group 55
Editis 56
Gameloft 59
Vivendi Village 61
*In Conclusion, How do Vivendi's Industrial and
  Financial Strategies Enable It to Offer Dividends to
  Its Shareholders? 63*

4 Vivendi's Political Profile   73
*Vivendi's Activities Raise Numerous Regulatory and
  Public Policy Issues 73*
Issues Related to Intellectual Property
  Rights Policies 73
Challenges Related to Competition Policy 74
Canal+, Vivendi and the French
  "Cultural Exception" 76
Vivendi's Governance 88
*Vincent Bolloré, His Personal and Family History and
  Links with the French Political Sphere 92*

5 Vivendi's Cultural Profile   98
*Vivendi, a Company Mainly Active in the Cultural
  and Media Economy 98*
*Aesthetic Issues Linked to Specific Socio-Economic
  Models 100*

*Cultural Dimension and Attempts to Influence
  the Political Public Space 101*
    Building the Image of a Corporate Citizen in
      Vivendi's Financial Communications 101
    The Many Controversies Surrounding
      Interventionism by Vivendi's Management 104
Conclusion 108
    What Is "Global" about an Industrial
      Player such as Vivendi? 108
    How Does Inclusion in a Company such as
      Vivendi Weigh on the Activities of the Cultural
      and Media Industries Brought Together under It? 109
    Is the Existence of a Large Financialized
      Corporation like Vivendi a Threat to Democracy? 110

Index 113

Acknowledgments

I received financial support from the Laboratory of Excellence: Cultural Industries and Artistic Creation (Labex ICCA) and the Laboratory of Information and Communication Sciences (LabSic) University Sorbonne Paris Nord.

I also thank Luis Albornoz and Maria Trinidad Garcia Leiva (Carlos III University of Madrid) for the support of the research program they lead: "Audiovisual Diversity and Online Platforms: Netflix as a case study" [CSO2017-83539-R], supported by the State Research Agency (AEI), within the National RDI Program Aimed at the Challenges of Society of the Spanish Ministry of Economy and Competitiveness, and the European Regional Development Fund (ERDF) of the European Union.

1 Introduction

Vivendi has a long history dating back to the first development of industrial capitalism in France in the 19th century. In the 1990s, driven by the wave of financialization and concentration linked to the speculative Internet "bubble", Vivendi grew considerably in Europe, but even more so in the United States, particularly through the acquisition of a large part of Universal's assets in the culture and media industries. Renamed Vivendi Universal in 1999, the company was then the world number two in this sector in terms of revenue. However, Vivendi Universal was one of the victims of the Internet bubble burst. The scope of the group was drastically reduced through asset sales and it narrowly avoided bankruptcy. Renamed Vivendi in 2003, the group then refocused on a smaller number of activities and lost a large part of its transnational dimension.

In 2020, Vivendi became the main French industrial player in the media and culture industries. At the end of 2019, it was positioned in the following segments: recorded music – via Universal Music Group (UMG); the television and cinematographic industry – via Canal+ Group; advertising (Havas Group); book publishing (Editis); video games (Gameloft); and entertainment and artistic activities – via Vivendi Village (talent management agencies, live performance venues, ticketing platform, etc.). Thus, it comprises a disparate set of industrial activities brought together under a subsidiary called "New initiatives", which notably includes the video-sharing site, Dailymotion, and activities in Africa via Group Vivendi Africa (GVA). Finally, it also has a set of financial holdings, including 23.4% of Telecom Italia, 28.80% of Mediaset (the audiovisual company run by the Berlusconi family) and 31.40% of an Indian player, Banijay Group Holding[1] (Vivendi, 2019: 6–7).

Vivendi has a rather limited revenue, which amounted to €15.898 billion in 2019. Of course, this makes it a small player when compared with the global digital giants. By way of example, Apple's revenue was $273.86 billion[2] in 2019, and those of Alphabet and Amazon $166.03 billion and $321.78 billion, respectively. These three players constitute partners of Vivendi in various respects, and especially in the distribution and promotion of its products. They are also competitors, however, since they offer video and recorded music services or books and other products also offered by Vivendi. Likewise, Vivendi's revenue is also small compared with the main global culture and media giants. Various global audiovisual players with which Vivendi is in a competitive or partnership relationship via its audiovisual subsidiary Canal+ Group have much higher turnovers. For example, The Walt Disney Company's revenue was $78.21 billion in 2019, while Netflix's amounted to $22.63 billion. Sony Corporation, the parent company of Sony Music, one of the two main competitors of Vivendi's music subsidiary, the UMG Group, achieved a turnover of 8,259 billion yen, or approximately $78.04 billion in 2019.[3] The difference in size is even greater when Vivendi is compared with players positioned in both different cultural and media industries and in the information and communication technology sector (ICT). Thus, AT&T had a turnover of $175.14 billion in 2019, having owned Time Warner – a major competitor of Vivendi Universal in the late 1990s – since 2018. Likewise, the 2019 turnover of Tencent, one of the Chinese giants to whom Vivendi sold 10% of the capital of the UMG Group in 2019, was $54.082 billion.[4]

That being said, Vivendi has a higher turnover than the other major French players in the culture and media industries, holding a dominant position, both industrially and financially, within the French culture and media capitalism in relation to other industrial players in this sector. Lagardère, which is one of Vivendi's main competitors, notably in book publishing via its subsidiary Hachette (the leading player in France), achieved a turnover of only €6.06 billion in 2019, while TF1, the largest advertising-financed television player in France, achieved sales of €2.08 billion.

Vivendi has a strong presence in Europe, with sales comparable to those of Bertelsmann, Europe's number one player in the cultural and media industries. The German giant is a major competitor to Vivendi in television (RTL Group owns the M6 television channel in France) and publishing (Penguin Random House), with a turnover of €18.02 billion in 2019.[5]

Vivendi is an interesting topic of study for several reasons, primarily because of the modes of transnationalization it employs and especially the oscillation between the French and foreign markets.

Vivendi has maintained its roots and remains under French management. As a company, it is therefore a representative case of many in the culture and media industries that have struggled to grow outside of their geographical area of origin. Its attempt to become a major player in the audiovisual industry in the US during the 1990s failed, as did its diversification into telecommunications in Europe and in emerging (Brazil) and developing countries (Morocco). It has not abandoned its transnational ambitions, however, and has broader geographical horizons than France and Europe. In 2019, the geographical breakdown of its revenue was as follows: 30.14% in France, 24.21% in the rest of Europe, 31.45% in North and South America, 9.80% in Asia and the Pacific, and 4.37% in Africa. As we will see later, this distribution differs greatly by activity. Vivendi has remained a global player because of its position as world leader in the recorded music industry. Other activities, such as audiovisual or book publishing, are less transnationalized. Productions in national languages by national creators still occupy a significant place. We will examine this question and particularly the issue linked to the deployment of digital platforms in the 2010s as well as the challenges this poses for Vivendi and its subsidiaries in these different sectors. Outside of France, the group also remains present in the rest of Europe and especially in Italy, as previously mentioned. Vivendi is the largest shareholder in Telecom Italia while it is a major minority shareholder in Mediaset, the audiovisual group controlled by Silvio Berlusconi. However, a question arises in this regard: what conditions favor or hamper Vivendi's transnationalization and internationalization strategies? The question is all the more relevant in Vivendi's case, since its domestic market, the French culture and media market, is only small compared with American or Chinese players. This puts Vivendi at a disadvantage, given that mastery of a large internal market has long been identified as a key factor in allowing the transnationalization of an industrial actor. The case of Netflix has further illustrated this.

A further question is whether Vivendi benefits from political protection? We will examine the extent to which its ancestors did in fact benefit from such protection. Since the 1980s and 1990s, the emergence and then development of the company have been supported by the French political authorities. Does Vivendi also benefit from so-called "cultural exception" policies? These public policies allow industrial players to benefit from various forms of aid, including public subsidies, but also result in markets being structured under the aegis of public authorities, in particular via various cross-subsidy mechanisms between socio-economic players. Authors such as Cowen (1998) have denounced the French "cultural exception" as economic protectionism in the name of defending cultural identity. Therefore, we ask whether the existence of both the "cultural exception" policy and a major national player like Vivendi promote the production and distribution of original national content.

A second reason for studying Vivendi is that, like various other players in the culture and media industries, it did not succeed in creating industrial synergies in the past. In other words, it failed to take advantage of its multiple positions in the various cultural sectors in either the 1990s (at its height, following its merger with Universal, Vivendi Universal was positioned in all sectors of the cultural industries as well as in portals and TV-cable and telecommunication networks), or in the 2010s, even if the group's reach was more limited during that decade.

The dominant reference in the 1980s, and especially the 1990s, was that of "convergence" between media and culture, telecommunications and ICT. This reference to convergence, which preceded the more contemporary digital age, has largely legitimized the vast movements of vertical integration and horizontal diversification in the culture and media industries which took place on both sides of the Atlantic in particular until the bursting of the Internet bubble in the early 2000s. In practice, however, in the absence of industrial synergies, no real convergence has taken place. The reference was thus purely rhetorical and ideological. We therefore pose the following questions: Are the industrial synergies between Vivendi's various subsidiaries becoming stronger in 2020? Or does Vivendi remain a conglomerate? And has the development of digital technology in its contemporary form, particularly via platforms, led to the strengthening of industrial synergies between the various sectors?

Vivendi is operating in a context of constant and profound industrial transformation linked to digitalization in the recorded music, pay television, publishing, video games, advertising, live entertainment and telecommunications sectors. One of the key points we address will relate to the deployment of digital platforms, and in particular streaming platforms, which are at the heart of changes in music and audiovisual production. The growing numbers of industrial actors positioned in various activities, from content to platforms and networks, in order to build "integrated players", is justified by the need to offer consumers a large range of exclusive and original content. It is the same argument that was made in the 1990s. In the possible absence of industrial synergies, then, should we consider the stakes of this positioning in several sectors to correspond to financial rather than industrial issues?

A third reason to study Vivendi, which is linked to the previous question, is to examine the financial strategies it employs. In recent years, the company has combined very tightly nested industry-related strategies and financial strategies. Ultimately, these strategies have been both industry-related and financial. In other words, acquisitions and disposals of assets have been undertaken not only with industrial objectives, but also as *"coups financiers"*, or high-risk financial operations, especially to benefit the reference shareholder, the Bolloré Group. Likewise, such financial maneuvers can turn into industrial operations when the opportunity arises, as shown by the example of Vivendi's rise within the capital of Lagardère (Lagardère is an important French company in the media industry) in 2020. Thus, Vivendi's trajectory is also a representative case of the ambiguous relationships that actors in the cultural industries have with major financial players. The company received strong support from such players in the 1990s, enabling Vivendi to finance very large acquisitions. However, in the 2000s, to cope with Vivendi's heavy debts, these financial players required the sale of very significant assets. Thus, one of the interests of studying Vivendi is to examine capitalist strategies in the culture and communication industries. What logic presides over the "centralization of capital" (Miège, 2000)? By centralization of capital, we mean the process through which acquisition operations reduce the number of "decision centers", or separate companies. Such movements to centralize capital can also lead to a reduced number of suppliers in the markets in which they occur. This question arises at the national level, especially in the case of Vivendi, whose manager Vincent Bolloré and his company are carrying out acquisition operations intended to either strengthen their presence in specific industrial fields or resell the acquired assets for a purely financial objective in the short or medium term. The question also has an impact at the transnational level. Why do the main transnational players not acquire smaller foreign players? Authors in the field of the political economy of communication, such as Herbert Schiller (1959, 1976) or Armand Mattelart (1979), consider national actors to be relays for transnational ones. The latter would therefore have more interest in contracting smaller players than in taking control. We will examine to what extent Vivendi acts as a relay for bigger and more transnationalized players. In addition, integration of the financial perspective will complement our analysis of transnational relations. To what extent do the major transnational players in the financial sphere (merchant banks, investment funds, financial rating agencies, etc.) have an interest in promoting capital transactions by medium-sized industrial players such as Vivendi?

Thus, in this book, we will present the main characteristics of Vivendi and put its strategies into perspective with more general trends in the cultural and media industries. Answers to the questions posed will be provided in four chapters devoted to the following issues:

- a history of the strategies adopted by the company, by its subsidiaries and the contextual elements that impacted on their development
- Vivendi's economic profile,
- political issues
- and cultural questions raised by Vivendi's positioning and strategies.

Methods and Sources

The methodology is inspired in the political economy of communication (PEC) approach and employs concepts from the theory of cultural industries. Thus, three levels of analysis will be put into perspective: Vivendi's industrial, financial and geographical structures and strategies; public policies and regulation that interfere with its activity; and trends in Vivendi's main markets and those of its subsidiaries. The book draws upon standard historical and documentary research from six types of primary and secondary source: (1) policy documents issued by various government entities or independent authorities; (2) corporate annual reports, quarterly reports, and other forms of trade-news releases publicly revealed by Vivendi and other related companies, such as the Bolloré Group; (3) news reports and analysis related to the industries in which Vivendi is positioned from financial and business sources and trade journals; (4) reports issued by professional investment analysts at banks, financial analysts and/or consultancy firms; (5) academic publications relating to industrial change, the transnationalization of culture or financialization; (6) interviews with Vivendi's managers or experts external to the company (regulatory authority officials, specialized journalists, etc.). The various possible biases will be analyzed as such, including reports from consulting firms linked to or remunerated by Vivendi, for example. Likewise, many documents issued directly by Vivendi will be considered not as reliable data but as financial communication, and will therefore be analyzed as such; that is to say, as attempts to construct favorable representations of the company's strategies.

Notes

1 Source: Vivendi, "Simplified economic organization chart of Vivendi", Activity Report 2919, 2019, 6–7.
2 Unless otherwise stated, all the data mentioned in this introduction on the turnover of these companies comes from Yahoo Finance.
3 Source: Sony Corporation, https://www.sony.net/SonyInfo/IR/library/presen/er/pdf/19q4_sonypre.pdf.
4 Source: Tencent, https://cdc-tencent-com-1258344706.image.myqcloud.com/uploads/2020/03/18/7fceaf3d1b264debc61342fc1a27dd18.pdf.
5 Source: Bertelsmann, https://www.bertelsmann.com/investor-relations/bertelsmann-at-a-glance/financial-figures/.

References

Cowen, Tyler, *In Praise of Commercial Culture*. Cambridge, MA: Harvard University Press, 1998.

Mattelart, Armand, *Multinational Corporations and the Control of Culture*. Sussex: Harvester Press, 1979.

Miège, Bernard, "À l'arrière-plan des récents mouvements de concentration", *Les dossiers de l'audiovisuel*, no. 94, 2000.

Schiller, Herbert, *Mass Communication and American Empire*. Boston, MA: Beacon Press, 1959.

Schiller, Herbert, *Communication and Cultural Domination*. Armonk, NY: M.E. Sharpe, 1976.

Vivendi, "Rapport d'activité annuel", 2019. https://www.vivendi.com/wp-content/uploads/2020/03/20200311-VIV_Vivendi-URD-2019.pdf.

2 Vivendi's History and Context

This chapter focuses on the history of Vivendi and those of its main subsidiaries, whether American, French or based in other countries. The objective will be to understand how the main contemporary characteristics of Vivendi are the legacy of the company's historical trajectories and those of its subsidiaries.

Vivendi was created through the agglomeration of several previously existing industrial players with separate histories and which do not have the same importance for the company and equal influences on its current dynamic. Henceforth, the reader can assume that the relationship with the French state, the relationship with the financial sphere and financial issues and arrangements for the organization of different industrial activities under the same capital complex comprise part of these "fundamental principles".

The "ancestors"

Vivendi's main "ancestor" was not active in either the media or cultural spheres. Rather, it was a French water supply company: Compagnie Générale des Eaux (CGE), founded over a century and a half ago. On 14 December 1853, an Imperial Decree[1] stipulated the details of a water concession from the city of Lyon to the Compagnie Générale des Eaux, founded that same year. The regulated tariffs would allow the company to generate significant profits, following which the scope of the Compagnie Générale des Eaux was extended far beyond the city of Lyon. CGE played a very important role in the history of French capitalism, especially because it had close relations with local authorities in particular cities. In addition to the water supply, CGE offered various other urban services (waste treatment, public parking and transportation, etc.). Therefore, the company forged a link between the financial and political spheres.

Vivendi's second great ancestor, Havas, is directly linked to the world of media. This company is even older than CGE, being founded on 22 October 1835, by a former banker, Charles-Louis Havas (1754–1858). In 1825, Havas founded his own translation agency, translating foreign news for the French press. In 1835, growing interest in international news led the entrepreneur to transform the company into the Havas Agency, which also supplied foreign newspapers with news from France. Throughout its history, the company had strong links with the French state, being founded after the revolution of 1830 under the "July Monarchy" (1830–1848) with the support of the French bourgeoisie. On the rise during the initial period of industrialization in France, this political regime attached great importance to industrial development. It also rapidly evolved toward a repressive regime, in particular regarding the workers' and republican movements. For both economic and political reasons, the July Monarchy attached great importance to information and its control. In 1838, the government asked Charles-Louis Havas to prepare a "ministerial correspondence" to keep state officials informed. In addition, the advent of the telegraph allowed the agency to develop while the press gradually benefited from three different evolutions in France: the "invention" of advertising by Emile de Girardin, which made it possible to lower the price of newspapers; the development of the railway, which made it possible to transport newspapers more easily; and finally a rise in literacy levels, which increased the number of potential readers.

From the middle of the 19th century onwards, the two sons and successors of Charles-Louis Havas reoriented the company's activity toward advertising. Through the acquisition of existing companies in particular, Havas then assumed a position of clear domination in the French advertising market, which was very dynamic thanks to the way the press was developing. Havas went through various stages in its development, including listing on the stock market when the Havas family ceded control in 1879, nationalization upon the end of the war in 1945, and finally, privatization in 1987.

Thus, throughout its history, Havas had advertising at its core but diversified into other fields, including tourism (this dating back to before the Second World War). From the late 1960s on, Havas expanded into communications consulting in the media, including the free press, and from the early 1970s, it made a move into the trade press, book publishing and pay television with Canal+.

Following privatization in 1987, Havas continued to develop and diversify, notably thanks to the 1991 acquisition of a major advertising player in France, RSCG, which also owned subsidiaries in the United States. In 1997, Havas absorbed the second largest French player in newspaper and book publishing, the company then named CEP (European Publishing Company) Communications. Havas already owned 40% of the capital of this company created in 1976. However, between 1976 and 1997, CEP Communications had grown considerably, along with Havas' control over its capital. In September 1997, Christian Brégou, the head of CEP Communications since its creation, was dismissed from his post and replaced by Havas CEO Pierre Dauzier. CEP Communications became Havas Publications Edition. CEP Communication is also the ancestor of Editis, a holding company for book publishers, which has also been under Vivendi since 2019.

In 1997, CGE began to hold a stake in Havas. Four different stages can be distinguished in the history of this group since the 1980s, as detailed below.

From the CGE to Vivendi: The Emergence of a Powerful Private Industrial Player in French Media and Culture in the 1980s

In the first stage, CGE bought up companies that were mainly active in the French market. The company first began its diversification into the cultural industries by buying assets in pay television. CGE acquired dominant positions on the three main levels of the sector: television channels, cable networks and production. In 1983, it took a 15% stake in Canal+, when the channel was first founded. Canal+ was the first pay-TV channel to be created in France and dominated the pay-TV sector in that country for a very long time, reaching a large audience and a large number of subscribers from its creation in 1984 until Netflix entered the French market in 2014. The Canal+ Group, with its various activities, is still one of Vivendi's main subsidiaries in 2020.

In addition to that participation, which constituted a minority holding at the time, CGE also developed a strategy of diversification in cable television networks, audiovisual production and even telecommunications. Thus, it implemented a so-called convergence strategy between culture, media and communication networks from the second half of the 1980s onwards. In 1984, CGE began its activity in cable networks through the creation of the Compagnie

Générale de Vidéo Communication. Later, this company, renamed NC Numericable, became one of the main actors in cable networks in France. In 1987, CGE established thematic television channels and developed television production activities in France by creating the company named La Générale d'Images. Going by the name of StudioCanal, in 2020 this company was one of the French and European leaders in film and television production. CGE also acquired or developed assets in mobile telecommunications. In 1987, it created SFR (the French Radio-telephony Company), which became the second largest French mobile operator. Then, the company bought assets in fixed telecommunications. In 1996, along with foreign players in the industry, CGE purchased a stake in Cegetel, at that time the second largest French fixed telecommunications operator and also the parent company of SFR.

In 1997, CGE took a decisive step forward by acquiring a first significant stake (21%) in the capital of Havas from the former major shareholder, Alcatel. In addition to the Havas shares it already held, this stake gave CGE a 29.3% share in Havas' capital. At the time, Havas was one of the most important French players in advertising, the main shareholder and co-founder of Canal+, and a major player in the book industry, second behind Hachette in France. At the same time, the company strengthened its investment in telecommunications. In July 1997, in partnership with SNCF, the French public railway company, CGE acquired a 49.9% stake in Télécom Développement (a long-distance network operating company) for €518 million.

In April 1998, CGE changed its name to Vivendi. Then, in May 1998, the company launched a public offer to exchange Havas shares for Vivendi shares. This successful transaction led to Havas being absorbed by Vivendi and the consolidation of Vivendi's stake in Canal+, which increased to 34%. Following its merger with Vivendi in 2000, Havas' former assets were transferred to a new segment of Vivendi called Vivendi Universal Publishing (VUP). However, VUP gradually withdrew from advertising activities, these having been allocated to a division called Havas Advertising Activities. In 2002, this company acquired the right to use the Havas name for the advertising activities carried out by VUP, anticipating the future sale of these activities. At the same time as it was carrying out these industrial operations, the company was also implementing major financial strategies. For example, in June 1998, Vivendi sold a 26.4% stake in the capital of Electrafina (a company that offered various services to local public authorities, including energy supply services) to Groupe Bruxelles Lambert S.A. for €1.1 billion.

At the end of this first stage, during which CGE transformed into Vivendi, we observe that four constants in the history of the group – four fundamental principles – were already in place. First, the close link with the French state, illustrating the great historical porosity between the state and the upper echelons of French capitalism. Second, the so-called convergence strategies between telecommunications, cable networks and cultural and media "content" were also already observable, as well as vertical integration on a capitalistic level. That said, the strategy did not lead to a real "convergence" between these activities, and in particular to vertical integrations at the industrial level. In other words, there were little or no exclusive relationships between the group's networks and its content. Various entities engaged in content and networks are juxtaposed within Vivendi, and this juxtaposition does not generate significant synergies. Thirdly, in the same way, the company was developing horizontal diversification strategies within media content itself, in particular by positioning itself in the audiovisual sector, the press and book publishing. Again, no industrial synergy emerged from these diversified positionings here. Fourth, the company was already implementing elements of financial strategies that are still in operation in 2020. On the one hand, the company was undertaking large and costly external growth operations. On the other hand, the company did not hesitate to sell assets it deemed to be non-strategic, using the cash to finance acquisitions. In short, with this dual financial strategy, CGE, which had just become Vivendi, already appeared both as an industrial group, developing industry-related strategies, and as a holding company whose reach was subject to incessant transformations aimed at fulfilling financial objectives. Depending on the acquisition or disposal opportunities that might arise, the company bought or sold assets for financial reasons.

From Vivendi to Vivendi Universal

In the second stage in its history, Vivendi continued its diversification in the cultural industries, but now internationally and particularly (but not exclusively) in the United States. It is then that the company became a truly global player. Meanwhile, it also strengthened its position in France, notably by increasing its investments in strategic companies in which it previously had a minority stake. Throughout its history, Vivendi has constantly aimed to own a 100% stake in its subsidiaries. The driving force behind this second step in the company's path came under the guidance of Jean-Marie Messier, who had already led the transformation of CGE into Vivendi. Messier became president of CGE in 1996, when he replaced Guy Dejouany.

Jean-Marie Messier is an emblematic member of the French technocratic elite. He does not hail from the industrial and financial Parisian higher bourgeoisie, but from a Catholic bourgeois family of the provinces, being born in Grenoble, a medium-sized city in the Alps, some 600 kilometers from Paris. His academic trajectory does reflect that of members of the French industrial, financial and political elites, however, having graduated from two of the three French *"grandes écoles"*: the Ecole Polytechnique, founded by Napoleon I, and the National School of Administration (ENA). The ENA was founded in 1945 with the mission of training and recruiting very senior public officials and some members of the political class. By way of example, three of the four French Presidents who succeeded François Mitterrand have been graduates of the ENA: Jacques Chirac, François Hollande and Emmanuel Macron. Valéry Giscard d'Estaing, president from 1974 to 1981 and defeated in the 1981 presidential elections by François Mitterrand was, like Jean-Marie Messier, a graduate of the Ecole Polytechnique and the ENA. The French ministerial cabinets are filled with ENA graduates and especially ones who topped the rankings in their year and could choose to be assigned to one of the three *"grand corps"*, which are prestigious and ancient inspection or jurisdictional institutions dating back to the times when France had a monarchy. Jean-Marie Messier chose the *"Inspection des Finances"*. The other two main bodies are the *"Conseil d'Etat"* and the *"Cour des Comptes"*. Most members of these institutions spend little time working in the institution they have joined. Rather, they very quickly enter ministerial positions. After a few years, they usually move into the private sector in positions of very high responsibility, as well as being awarded places on the boards of directors of large French companies. As a result, the French technocratic elites at the head of state and private companies are very homogeneous. Their members know each other well, because they almost all come from the same *Grandes Ecoles* or *grands corps*, and especially the *Inspection des Finances*. This is important to know if we are to understand how in France the industrial and financial spheres and the higher spheres of the French state are closely interwoven. Thus, the distinction between the private and the public sector has only a relative significance in France. CGE, Havas and Vivendi, which all followed public policies by carrying out actions encouraged by the state and in return used the state to carry out their own industry-related and financial strategies, are clear examples of this. This close interweaving also helps to explain why Jean-Marie Messier was able to take very important decisions with few checks and balances.

In 1996, when Jean-Marie Messier became head of CGE, the policy of horizontal diversification had deepened. Vivendi was at this point adopting important positions in new activities as well as in those in which the company was already positioned. In 1998, Vivendi initiated its activities in video games via the acquisition of Cendant Software (a publisher of educational software and games in the United States) for €678 million. Diversification came in different forms, such as, for example, investment in live performance halls. Thus, in June 2001, Vivendi acquired the Olympia, a very famous and important venue in the history of variety music performance in Paris. Likewise, Vivendi also acquired international players in the audiovisual industry, with several major acquisitions being carried out.

The first was the transaction with Pathé, a major historical French player in the film industry, which also holds assets abroad. This operation was complex and typical of the interweaving of financial and industrial dimensions found in Vivendi's strategies, but also of the importance the group attaches to its development in online portals and abroad. In January 1999, Vivendi and Canal+ together acquired 29.9% of Pathé's capital. In June of that same year, Pathé's director, Jérôme Seydoux, proposed a merger. This operation was carried out on the basis of share exchanges – with a parity of three Vivendi shares for two Pathé shares – and by means of a capital increase. On this occasion, Vivendi issued 26 million shares at a value of €1.9 billion. This merger was immediately followed by a split. Vivendi retained Pathé's stake in Canal Satellite (20%) and BSkyB (17%), while Pathé (in fact, the Fornier company owned by the Seydoux family) invested in cinema activities (theaters, distribution and production), thematic channels, the Libération newspaper and Olympique Lyonnais sports club. Fornier only retained 2% of Vivendi's capital, while Vivendi retained Pathé's stakes in the two leading European satellite television companies: 17% of the BSkyB bouquet in the United Kingdom, valued at around €2.59 billion, and 20% of Canal Satellite in France, valued at €229 million. In addition, Fornier paid Vivendi €520.9 million in cash to buy back the assets previously sold in the merger. This operation is therefore representative of the strategies being conducted by Vivendi with its capital at the time, enabling it to acquire assets by increasing capital. In addition, following this transaction, Canal+ held 90% of the capital of Canal Satellite. A strategy was then implemented to move toward 100% ownership of all subsidiaries. In July 1999, Vivendi acquired Pearson and Granada' interests in BSkyB, which amounted to 7% of the capital, resulting in Vivendi holding 24.5% of BSkyB. These operations took place after the failure of negotiations with Rupert Murdoch on the proposed merger of Canal+ and BSkyB in March 1999.

The second strategy involved Vivendi launching online portals. In May 2000, Vivendi and Vodafone reached an agreement to create an equally owned joint venture, including Canal+. It was given the name Vizzavi, and was an online portal available in most European countries. A further example was the creation of Pressplay in February 2001, a joint venture with Sony aimed at providing subscription online music. This portal was designed to offer subscribers content produced by Vivendi's subsidiaries via a multimedia solution (that is to say, on computers, phones, music players and televisions). At the same time, the world leader in media and entertainment, as well as Internet access, AOL Time Warner, was developing exactly the same strategy of offering proprietary content. This strategy implied a vertical integration in all sectors of media and entertainment via the acquisition of strong positions in the networks (Internet access, fixed and mobile telephony, cable networks). Such strategies were encouraged by the major players in the financial sphere (Bouquillion, 2008). In this period of the so-called "New Economy", the future of media and entertainment was also described by experts as necessarily being tied to networks.

A third transaction was to take place in December 2000, in the form of the large-scale operation so desired by Jean-Marie Messier: a merger with Seagram, one of the leading American players in the media industry, and particularly cinema with Universal Studios and recorded music with MCA and Polygram. Seagram shares were acquired in exchange for Vivendi-Universal shares. It was at this point that Vivendi became Vivendi Universal. Indeed, in December 2000, following the acquisition of 100% of Canal+ and the Seagram merger, Vivendi-Universal was incorporated. Former shareholders in Canal+, Seagram and Vivendi received shares in the new company, Vivendi Universal, in exchange for their shares in the aforementioned three companies. In December 2001, Seagram's assets in wines and spirits were sold for $8.1 billion. This first large-scale purchase transaction in the United States was completed a year later when, in December 2001, Vivendi acquired an additional 50% stake in USA Networks – an important actor in the American audiovisual industry – leading to it holding 93% of the capital. At this point, Jean-Marie Messier's main objective seemed to have been achieved: Vivendi owned content in the United States and networks in Europe to distribute such content.

A fourth strategy saw Vivendi-Universal carry out various diversification operations in either content or networks in different regions. More than a constructed strategy, Vivendi-Universal was taking advantage of the acquisition opportunities that arose. For example, in August 1999, Vivendi acquired the medical publisher MediMedia for €237 million. In the same year, Aique (a publisher of books and school articles in Argentina) and Atica & Scipione (a publisher of books and school articles in Brazil) were acquired. Likewise, acquisitions were carried out in the networks in territories in which the company had little presence. For example, in 2000, United Telecoms Investment (Hungary) was acquired for €128 million, as was a 40% stake in Kencell Communications Limited (Kenya), for €36 million. Most of these acquisition opportunities had little industrial interest because they did not allow the creation of synergies with the industrial activities already integrated within the company. They did offer financial opportunities, however. For example, in May 2004, Vivendi announced the sale of its stake in Kencell, the aforementioned Kenyan mobile phone subsidiary, for $230 million, which represented a very significant capital gain over the purchase price.[2] The company also strengthened its position in telecommunications, especially in countries formerly colonized by France and where French influence was still important. For example, in 2001, Vivendi acquired a stake in Maroc Telecom (operating telephony services in Morocco) for €2.4 billion. Meanwhile, other transactions were more consistent with the strategies deployed by Vivendi Universal, particularly in those territories defined as priority. For example, in December 1999, a 49% stake was acquired in a joint venture (TELCO) with Elektrim (a mobile telephony and cable telephony network operator in Poland) for €1.2 billion.

A fifth strategy entailed Vivendi increasing its stake in the capital of its French subsidiaries in which it did not yet hold 100%. In October 1999, Vivendi organized an exchange of shareholdings: Richemont gave Vivendi 15% of Canal+'s capital, and in return, Richemont received a 2.9% stake in Vivendi. Thanks to this exchange, Vivendi held 49% of Canal+. Likewise, in June 2001, 100% of StudioCanal's capital became controlled by the Canal+ Group after a takeover bid. At the same time, Vivendi's interest in the capital of MultiThématiques, a package of channels for cable and satellite created with Lagardère, increased to 64%. In 2001, Vivendi acquired the sports club Paris Saint-Germain (soccer) as well as 100% ownership of NC Numericable, the largest French cable network. These acquisitions were partially financed by the sale of minority interests held in various companies. For example, in January 2001, Canal+ sold stakes in Eurosport France (39%) and Eurosport International (49.5%) to TF1 (then and still in 2020, the main channel financed by advertising in France) for €300 million. These stakes had been acquired in parity with TF1 from ESPN in February 2000 for an amount of €80 million. Therefore, Vivendi made excellent financial gains through these operations.

A sixth strategy saw purely financial operations being carried out. For example, in July 1999, an investment fund called @Viso was formed. It was funded for a total of $100 million by Vivendi and SoftBank (Japanese venture capital funds). At the same time, Vivendi contributed $200 million to the Softbank Capital Partners investment fund and Newscorp International $100 million (it had a total value of $1.8 billion). These financial operations were undertaken on a transnational scale in collaboration with major foreign players. Along with its diversification in entertainment and telecommunications, Vivendi sold assets related to its former activities. In 1996–1997, Vivendi sold its health activities. Then the company gradually sold its shares in Vivendi Environnement. In 2000, Vivendi Environnement was separately incorporated and listed on the stock exchange. This subsidiary included the oldest CGE activities (urban services, energy, transport, waste management, real estate and construction). In December 2001, Vivendi Universal owned 63% of Vivendi Environnement, in June 2002, 47.7%, and by December 2002, only 20.4%. In 2003, Vivendi Environnement was renamed Veolia Environnement and, in December 2004, Vivendi Universal sold most of its lasting stake in Veolia.

The end of this second stage was characterized by significant acquisitions, as Vivendi Universal became multi-positioned in almost any content (broadcasting, books, music, media, and games). At that time, the company was the second largest global player in the entertainment industry. However, after the bursting of the financial bubble in the early 2000s, this large conglomerate sold many of its assets, ushering in the third stage in its history.

Back to Vivendi: The Company Came Close to Bankruptcy but Multiplied Sales and Acquisitions

The fourth stage in Vivendi's history began after the stock market crash of 2001. At that time, the company was experiencing great financial difficulties. This stage is characterized by the coexistence of significant divestments of activities for financial gain and acquisitions for industrial purposes. Vivendi Universal's severe financial crisis was partly due to purely financial reasons. Indeed, Vivendi has often paid high prices for its acquisitions. In the late 1990s, companies in the culture and communication industries were overvalued. In addition, Vivendi's acquisitions were not only financed by exchanges of shares or capital increases, but also debt. Therefore, the company had a large amount of debt and the interest rate on its debt was increasing, leading to Vivendi Universal's debt being poorly rated by credit ratings agencies. On the other hand, industrial synergies between the various components of the company were very low. Jean-Marie Messier's strategy of articulating networks in Europe (telecommunications, satellite packages, cable networks, Internet access, premium channels) with American content had failed, leaving Vivendi Universal close to bankruptcy. The company even had trouble finding short-term bank financing to pay suppliers and employees. Messier was forced to leave his post in 2002, a year in which Vivendi Universal reported losses of €23.3 billion and debts of €25.1 billion.

At this point, two new leaders began to play a central role. The first was the Chairman of the Supervisory Board, Jean-René Fourtou, who, unlike Messier, had a background in business and not one of a high public official. Although his prior experience was completely alien to Vivendi Universal's areas of business in media and entertainment, he had a reputation for being a good financier. Fourtou was placed at the head of the company, thanks to the support of Jean-Claude Bébéar, who created and managed the leading French insurance firm, AXA. Bébéar was at that time considered one of the most influential figures of French capitalism, and he is often blamed for the fall of Jean-Marie Messier. Vivendi Universal's financial situation was so poor that influential decision makers in the financial sphere had a *de facto* say over the life or death of the company. Therefore, their influence over the board of directors was such that they were able to appoint new directors as replacements for Jean-Marie Messier's team. Thus, Jean-René Fourtou's initial main role was to reassure financial circles that they would continue to grant cash advances to the company. Ultimately, however, his role was also to restore the structural solvency of the company. In light of this, he set up a debt-relief program that led to many assets being sold to avoid bankruptcy.

The other leader, who had a more executive role, was Jean-Bernard Lévy. This important figure in French industry (in 2020, he was the director of the historic French electricity company, EDF) is a graduate of the Ecole Polytechnique and an Engineer in the telecommunications "*corps*". He was a senior civil servant and held important positions within the historic French telecommunications operator (France Telecom, now Orange) before joining Vivendi Universal. At that time, France Telecom was a body of the public administration. Under Lévy's direction, Vivendi Universal recovered it after the departure of Jean-Marie Messier and defined new industry-related strategies for its growth. Meanwhile, it withdrew from film activities in the United States, increased its stake in SFR, purchased Activision, merged with Blizzard and acquired and developed Global Village Telecom (GVT), the Brazilian Internet broadband leader. Viewed as a whole, Jean-Bernard Lévy pursued a dual logic: sell assets in the United States acquired under Jean-Marie Messier and all assets outside the media and ICTs; and acquire assets in telecommunications, video games and the audiovisual sector, either in France or in emerging countries considered as promising, such as Brazil or Morocco.

In 2002, there were major sales of subsidiaries and participations, including: Vivendi Universal Publishing (the second largest French player in the book and news industries); Houghton Mifflin; 11% of Echo Star; 44% of Cegetel and Telepiu (satellite TV in Italy). Similarly, in 2004, Vivendi Universal Entertainment (VUE) was sold to General Electric, before being renamed NBC-Universal and becoming a joint venture 80% owned by General Electric and 20% by Vivendi Universal. Vivendi finally sold its 20% stake between 2009 and 2011. Consequently, Vivendi Universal withdrew from the press and book industries, both in the United States and Europe, and the audiovisual industry in the United States. Similarly, most of Canal+'s international subsidiaries were also sold. Almost all of these companies or Vivendi Universal's shares in them were sold at lower prices than the purchase price. Vivendi Universal primarily sold companies that were unprofitable or those for which a buyer came forward. The telecommunications subsidiaries that provided a significant cash flow were retained during this period and played a prominent role in the financial restructuring of Vivendi Universal.

Alongside these divestitures, during this period Vivendi Universal conducted different acquisitions for industrial purposes, strengthening its investment in a few sectors considered priority to acquire or maintain a leading position. The company also strengthened in certain countries in which it already had an established presence (especially France) and in high-growth emerging countries like Brazil. In addition, it pursued its historical strategy of increasing control over its most strategic subsidiaries, if possible up to 100%. Thus, Vivendi developed its position in telecommunications: in 2003, it increased its ownership stake in Cegetel (70%), before in 2008, SFR, Vivendi Universal's mobile telecommunications subsidiary, took control of the remaining 29.90% Cegetel shares it did not yet own, meaning Cegetel became 100% owned by SFR. Meanwhile, in 2004 Vivendi Universal took a 51% control in Maroc Telecom, following this with a $2.8 billion takeover of GVT in 2009. By 2010, it controlled almost 100% of GVT. In June 2011, Vivendi increased its shareholding in SFR by purchasing a 44% stake for €7.75 billion. The company also strengthened its position in pay television, mainly in France, acquiring assets in audiovisual production and pay channel packages. From 2005 to 2007, Vivendi took control of the television network TPS, which was its only competitor in satellite channel satellite packages in France. Then, in 2011, the Canal+ Group acquired a 33% stake in Orange Cinema Series, the French telecom operator's movie channel package, while also acquiring the free-to-air television channels of the Bolloré Group. In December 2009, the Canal+ Group bought a 10% stake in Canal+ France, which was previously owned by TF1. In February 2010, Vivendi acquired another 5.1% stake in Canal+ France. With these two transactions, Vivendi held 80% of Canal+ France (via the Canal+ Group, a wholly owned subsidiary of Vivendi). In addition, the company also strengthened its position in the music industry. In 2006–2007, Vivendi bought the music publishing activities belonging to BMG, BMG Music Publishing (BMGP). Through this operation, which cost €1.63 billion, Universal Music became the world leader in music publishing. In November 2011, UMG then bought EMI Recorded Music for £1.2 billion. And by the late 2000s, Vivendi had strengthened to become the world leader in video games production. In July 2008, Activision Blizzard was created through the merger of the two entities Activision and Blizzard Entertainment.

After taking back its name in 2006, Vivendi would follow this dual strategy of sales and acquisitions for the next ten years. However, at the end of this third stage in its history, the company remained highly indebted. In addition, its positioning was so diverse that it had become a conglomerate. Thus, pressures were felt to dismantle Vivendi, particularly from the financial sector. Indeed, demands were being made by decision makers in the financial sphere for the company to be sold on a breakup basis, or at least split, because, according to experts writing at the time:

> Vivendi is worth less on the stock market than the sum of its very promising components: the telecom operators SFR (France), Maroc Telecom and GVT; the music publisher Universal Music; the pay channel Canal+ and the world leader in video games Activision Blizzard.
>
> (AFP&Reuters, 2012)

In April 2012, its share price was so low that rumors suggested raiders would seize the company. However, a famous French businessman, Vincent Bolloré, would soon take advantage of the low price to acquire a large shareholding in the company.

Vivendi: A Player in the Media Sector or Various Assets for Sale?

This period was characterized by a change in the management of the company and at the industrial level via the rationalization of Vivendi's scope and the company finally being split in two. This fifth stage in Vivendi's history began in 2012 when Jean-Bernard Lévy, joint head with Jean-René Fourtou, was dismissed. Fourtou had instigated Vivendi's telecommunications policy, the sector that provided the company with a significant cash flow and allowed it to avoid bankruptcy. However, in 2011, SFR, Vivendi's main asset in telecommunications, saw its financial results deteriorate sharply, Jean-Bernard Lévy's policy of developing the telecommunications arm appearing to have failed. Jean-René Fourtou played a central role in ousting Jean-Bernard Lévy, considering the industrial synergies between the various components of the company to be too weak. He even proposed dividing the company into two or even three distinct entities. In any event, Lévy's resignation saw the Vivendi share price rise sharply.

As previously mentioned, in 2012 Vincent Bolloré began to play an important role in shareholding and progressively in the management of Vivendi, taking advantage of the historically very low price of Vivendi shares to acquire significant stakes in Vivendi capital from April 2012 onwards. Rumors of raids were numerous. It should be remembered that Bolloré was himself renowned for various hostile attempts to take control of several companies, including TF1.

In the latter case, despite failing to take control, he had made very significant financial gains, thanks to the operation. The position of Bolloré's company, the Bolloré Group, strengthened quickly within Vivendi's capital. In September 2012, the Canal+ Group took control of two television channels belonging to the Bolloré Group: Direct8 and Direct Star. In return, Bolloré obtained 1.7% of Vivendi's capital. Thanks to this stake, which was in addition to the shares it already held, the Bolloré Group became Vivendi's largest shareholder, with a 4.41% stake. The following year, in 2013, the Bolloré Group further increased its stake to hold 5% of the capital. It was then that Vincent Bolloré sought to take over the management of Vivendi. The rivalry between Vincent Bolloré and Jean-René Fourtou then developed, although initially the two men were forced to find compromises, neither of the two being able to survive without the other. A transitional period therefore began. In September 2013, while Jean-René Fourtou was trying to appoint a German, Thomas Rabe, then chairman of Bertelsmann, as head of Vivendi, Vincent Bolloré himself ran for the post of chairman of Vivendi's management board, which confers effective control over the management of the company. This takeover would not come until a little later, however.

In September 2013, Fourtou and Bolloré agreed to split Vivendi into two components: on the one hand, there was the main telecommunications asset, SFR, then the French number two in telephony, which was to be sold; and, on the other, there were the media and entertainment activities, together with the Brazilian Internet service provider GVT, which were to remain part of the company and be placed under the leadership of Bolloré. Keeping GVT within Vivendi surprised experts, who noted that it was not a player in the media industry. In fact, GVT remained within the scope of the group because Vivendi management believed it could be sold at a very good price at a later date. A few months before the split, Vivendi had decided not to sell GVT because the price offered by the potential buyers was below Vivendi's valuation of 7 to 8 billion euros (Cuny, 2013b). Bolloré also became vice-chairman of Vivendi's supervisory board, with Fourtou remaining chairman. This clearly illustrates the importance and persistence of the financial dimension in Vivendi's history. The presence of such an asset within the company is not explained only or sometimes not at all by industrial logic (i.e. due to synergies with the other components of the company), but by financial reasoning: the possibility of acquiring an asset at a price considered low with the hope of subsequently reselling it for a significant gain.

Finally, the rivalry between Fourtou and Bolloré ended in June 2014. The latter became chairman of the supervisory board, while the former was appointed honorary chairman. This decision allowed Bolloré to take power while allowing Fourtou – considered in the financial sphere as an expert in "good" financial management – to keep a position at the company. Bolloré also paid tribute to Fourtou, saying that thanks to his actions Vivendi was in "an extremely favorable balance sheet situation". The company had accumulated €2 billion in net cash by the end of 2014, despite being near to bankruptcy when Jean-Marie Messier was ousted. For his part, Fourtou insisted that Bolloré was not a senior civil servant but a "true" industrialist: "Vincent Bolloré is an enterprising industrialist, imaginative, tenacious, and one who has a sense of the shareholder's interests [...]". He also declared that the increase in Vivendi's share price over the previous two years had been largely due to Bolloré's investments within Vivendi's capital (Cuny, 2014). Bolloré appointed Arnaud de Puyfontaine – a trusted ally – as chairman of the board of directors. De Puyfontaine was previously the leader of the Hearst press and television group and knew the American market well.

This new period was also characterized by the rationalizing of Vivendi's scope in terms of two main activities in the cultural industries. First, the company chose to focus on the audiovisual industries – mainly pay-tv through the Canal+ Group. Second, Vivendi retained its position in recorded music, especially thanks to UMG, a legacy from the period when Jean-Marie Messier ran the company. Before Netflix established itself on the French market from 2014 onwards, Vivendi was the French leader in pay-tv, and the world leader in recorded music. This rationalization occurred through very significant asset sales. SFR was sold, as announced upon conclusion of the agreement between Fourtou and Bolloré. In November 2014, an agreement was reached between Vivendi and Numericable, the main French cable television operator, for the sale of 80% of the capital of SFR to the latter for an amount of €13 billion – the largest transaction to take place in France in 2014. In February, the remaining 20% were sold to Numericable for a further €3.9 billion. With this, a new major player in the French culture and communication industries was created, Numericable-SFR, which goes by the name of Altice in 2020. Back in 2014, two months prior to the sale, an agreement had been reached between Vivendi and Telefonica for the sale of GVT. Vivendi received €4.66 billion in cash, from which €450 million of bank debt were deducted. In addition, Telefonica also transferred to Vivendi 5.7% of the capital of Telecom Italia, whose market value was €1.01 billion on September 18, as well as 7.4% of the capital of Telefonica Brasil, valued at €2.02 billion (Barzic, 2014). When the transaction was finalized in May 2015, Vivendi exchanged part of its shares in Telefonica Brasil for shares in Telecom Italia, thus receiving 8.3% of the shares of the historic Italian telecommunications operator. The sale of GVT brought in approximately €7.5 billion for Vivendi, which roughly corresponded to Vivendi's financial capital gains expectations. In May 2014, Vivendi was able to finalize the sale of its 53% stake in Maroc Telecom to the Emirati operator Etisalat. Thanks to this transaction, which was initiated in 2013, Vivendi earned €4.13 billion. In July 2013, the company announced the sale of most (85%) of its 61.1% stake in Activision Blizzard, the video game production "giant", which notably produced Call of Duty and Warcraft. That sale brought in $8.2 billion. In January 2016, Vivendi announced the sale of the remaining shares for an amount of $1.1 billion.

Vivendi was strengthened through this refocusing on media and entertainment and the improvement of its financial situation. Thus, the new head of the company decided to further pursue its strategy in the media and entertainment sector and capitalize on industrial synergies, as he underlined when he took office as chairman of the supervisory board:

> The strategy has been clearly established. It is about transforming this company, which was a financial holding, into an industrial integrated group in terms of content. It is an ambitious project, because we face more powerful foreign competitors hunting for prey [...] There is a hidden value: there are all the convergences, all the synergies. By combining all of these activities, we can generate much more value. Let me explain: Canal Plus would have difficulty launching itself in the American market, the main television market, but it could save a lot of time by relying on the skills of Universal, which is a legend in America. GVT, which has undergone extraordinary development, can also call on Universal. This is all Vivendi's commitment to the future, based on three entities that may seem a little disparate.
>
> (Vincent Bolloré, quoted in Cuny, 2014)

Regardless of this commitment to industry, it appeared that not only were these asset disposals intended to rationalize Vivendi's industrial scope, but they must first generate cash. According to experts, the proceeds from these disposals were intended to repay the significant debts that Vivendi had contracted: "With the two disposals of Maroc and Activision (totalling €10.4 billion), Vivendi will almost erase its net debt (€13.2 billion at the end of March 2013)" (Cuny, 2013a). In order to support the Vivendi share price on the stock market, management redistributed a significant portion of the proceeds from these disposals in telecommunications and video gaming to shareholders.

By way of conclusion to this chapter on the history of Vivendi, a new era appeared to open up for the company in the mid-2010s with the refocusing on media and entertainment and the coming to power of Vincent Bolloré. However, it would still be faced with the same central question it had faced since Compagnie Générale des Eaux diversified and became Vivendi: whether to rationalize its activities around a core of business that would be clearly identified and limited, or to diversify and seek external growth.

Notes

1 At that time, France was ruled by an emperor, Napoleon III Bonaparte, grand-nephew of Napoléon I. Napoleon III is very influenced by a philosophical and political doctrine, Saint-Simonianism, which was founded by a thinker named Claude-Henri de Rouvroy de Saint-Simon (1760–1825). Saint-Simonianism pleads in particular in favor of the advent of an industrialized society in which public authorities, industries and engineers would go hand in hand. Networks are seen as a key element of industrialization.
2 Businesswire, "Vivendi Universal Announces Sale of Its Interest in Kencell for $230 Million", 25 May 2004. https://www.businesswire.com/news/home/20040525005764/en/Vivendi-Universal-Announces-Sale-Interest-Kencell-230

References

AFP&Reuters, "Jean-Bernard Lévy quitte la présidence de Vivendi", *Le Monde*, 28 juin 2012. https://www.lemonde.fr/economie/article/2012/06/28/vivendi-jean-bernard-levy-sur-le-depart_1726082_3234.html

Barzic, Gwénaëlle, "Vivendi signe la vente de l'opérateur GVT à Telefonica", *Challenges*, 19 September, 2014. https://www.challenges.fr/high-tech/vivendi-signe-la-vente-de-l-operateur-gvt-a-telefonica_140925

Bouquillion, Philippe, *Les industries de la culture et de la communication. Les stratégies du capitalisme.* Grenoble: Presses Universitaires de Grenoble, 2008.

Cuny, Delphine, "Vivendi vend ses jeux vidéo Activision Blizzard", *La Tribune*, 26 July 2013(a).

Cuny, Delphin, "Vivendi : l'inévitable session", *La Tribune*, 11 September, 2013(b). https://www.latribune.fr/technos-medias/20130911trib000784482/vivendi-l-inevitable-scission.html

Cuny, Delphine, "La stratégie de Bolloré: créer des synergies au sein du nouveau Vivendi", *La Tribune*, 24 June, 2014. https://www.latribune.fr/technos-medias/20140624trib000836742/la-strategie-de-bollore-creer-des-synergies-au-sein-du-nouveau-vivendi.html

3 Vivendi's Economic Profile

The central question in this chapter concerns the main industrial and financial dynamics of a large transnational company active in the media and entertainment industry such as Vivendi. Are its objectives primarily industrial? In this case, then a company like Vivendi would aim to gather various components together to create synergies despite sector differences. Or are its goals primarily financial? In this scenario, by contrast, the diverse industrial positions adopted by the company would result from a succession of opportunities for acquisitions of external companies and divestments. The main challenge would be to maximize the distribution of dividends for shareholders through multiple and moving games of asset acquisitions and disposals. Should we therefore see industrial and financial issues as opposed, considering that the pursuit of strictly financial interests would lead a company such as Vivendi to commit to short-term financial speculation and prevent it from making a long-term commitment to industry? The question we pose here, then, revolves around the challenges of financialization at a time when industrial players, including companies active in the media and entertainment, like Vivendi, are involved in financialization because they are listed on the stock exchange. Does this mean that industrial prospects are being ignored in favor of financial requirements and that all of the company's resources are being used to satisfy shareholders, to the detriment of industrial investments?

In order to provide some answers to this question, we must first examine the acquisition and sale transactions carried out by Vivendi, and second, analyze the industrial logic on which the various Vivendi subsidiaries are based in order to study whether they present cross-functional lines and synergies or, contrarily, are compartmentalized. And in a third and final phase, we will need to examine how Vivendi is able to offer dividends to its shareholders through the industrial and financial strategies it has implemented.

Under the Leadership of Vincent Bolloré and His Group, Vivendi Is Experiencing a Strong Expansion Phase

Vivendi's scope decreased sharply in the previous period (from 2002 onwards, and even more after the company split at the end of 2013). Vivendi had refocused on two different activities: pay television and recorded music, but experienced a new phase of expansion from 2015 onwards after the Bolloré Group and its emblematic manager, Vincent Bolloré, took over, resulting in numerous significant acquisitions and disposals of assets. Some of these transactions took place in industrial sectors in which Vivendi was already strongly positioned, including the audiovisual sector. Others occurred in sectors in which Vivendi had held positions in the past, such as books and video games.

Vivendi Acquires Audiovisual Assets

From 2015 onwards, Vivendi carried out a fairly disparate set of operations comprising both 100% acquisitions of external companies and others that combined industrial alliances and acquisitions of capital investments. These operations were implemented both in France and abroad. Between April and September 2015, Vivendi bought the DailyMotion online video platform (described as a French-speaking YouTube) from the incumbent French telecommunications operator, Orange. It also acquired French production companies, or took stakes in them. These transactions included a 26% stake in the capital of Banijay, a large French company headed by self-made businessman Stéphane Courbit. This equity investment resulted in a long-term partnership. In October 2019, Banijay bought out the leading European production company, Endemol Shine, and thus became the world's largest television producer. Although the cost of the acquisition has been kept secret, experts believe it may have been around 2 billion euros. Endemol's debt was around $1.6 billion. This new player was expected to achieve a turnover of around 3 billion euros and thus triple Banijay's revenues. Since completion of the transaction, Banijay and Endemol have been jointly owned by a financial holding company controlled by Stéphane Courbit LDH (67.1%) and Vivendi (32.9%). Endemol was previously owned by The Walt Disney Company and the Apollo Global Management investment fund, and was put on sale in July 2018 at a price of between €2.3 billion and €3 billion (La

Tribune, 2019). Likewise, in 2016, StudioCanal, a subsidiary of the Canal+ Group, acquired a stake in three independent production companies: 33% of the capital of the Spanish Bambu Producciones and 20% of the British Urban Myth Films and Sunny March TV (Ridet & Cassini, 2016).

In April 2016, a so-called strategic partnership agreement was concluded with Mediaset, the Italian television group owned by Silvio Berlusconi and his family. Vivendi acquired 3.5% of the Italian company's capital and 100% of that of Mediaset Premium (an Italian pay channel package). In exchange, Vivendi transferred 3.5% of its own capital to Mediaset. The stated objective of this operation was to initiate a pooling of the audiovisual assets of the two groups, Vivendi and Mediaset, in order to launch a "European Netflix". The agreement also provided for collaborations between pay-TV channels Canal+ and Mediaset Premium in an attempt to save on the costs of purchasing broadcasting rights for sporting events and purchasing or producing original content. In 2016, despite having been in existence for ten years and having spent significant sums (€710 million) to buy the 2015–2018 broadcasting rights of the Champions League (soccer), Mediaset Premium had only 1.3 million customers. Mediaset's pay channel package was lagging far behind the Sky Italia package belonging to News Corporation, which had 4.7 million customers (Ridet & Cassini, 2016). However, relations between the heads of the two companies quickly became confrontational. In December 2016, Vivendi launched a hostile takeover bid for Mediaset, becoming its second largest shareholder, with 28.8% of the capital and nearly 30% of voting rights (De Laubier, 2020). Vivendi's aim was to wrestle control of Mediaset from Fininvest, the holding company belonging to the Berlusconi family and largest shareholder. In 2016, Mediaset, historically the main player in private advertising-funded television in Italy, controlled 57% of the television advertising market in that country. As early as March 2016, the major Italian daily newspaper *La Repubblica* announced that Vivendi's objective was to obtain full control of Mediaset, Mediaset Premium being heavily indebted and presenting only weak prospects for growth (Pons, 2016). In addition, an exchange of shares at parity (3% of Vivendi's share capital for 3% of that of Mediaset) seemed unattractive, because the two groups had very different capitalizations. At the time of the deal, Vivendi's stock market valuation was €25.5 billion and that of Mediaset was only €4.3 billion. The sale of Mediaset Premium shares would compensate only very partially for this disparity. Indeed, the company had never even reached breakeven point (ibid.). Thus, the interest of the operation clearly lay elsewhere for Vivendi. In 2020, hostilities between Fininvest and Bolloré have not ceased, and its minority stake does not allow Vivendi to control Mediaset, which has remained under the control of Fininvest. In February 2020, the latter controlled 39.53% of the capital and 41.09% of the voting rights.

Vivendi is notably opposed to the plan to create a "European holding company MediaForEurope" (MFE). This new entity, which is to be based in Amsterdam and listed on the Stock Exchanges in Italy and Spain, was approved at a general meeting of Mediaset on 4 September 2019. MFE is expected to combine the Italian and Spanish activities of Mediaset, while owning the 15.1% stake Mediaset inherited in the German audiovisual group ProSiebenSat.[1] Media. The latter is MFE's first European partner, and has the aim of developing the future Over The Top (OTT) video platform, currently nicknamed by certain media as "Euroflix" (at one time referred to as "Latin Netflix") (ibid.). A holding under Dutch law, MFE has the stated objective of creating a European champion in content distribution. However, many experts believe that its primary objective is to allow the Berlusconi family to tighten its control over Mediaset. So far, Vivendi has succeeded in preventing the operation from going ahead, courts in Spain and the Netherlands having blocked the MFE project (Manière, 2020a).

A further dispute between the two companies is still ongoing in 2020. Mediaset has filed a complaint with AGCom, the Italian communications regulator, accusing Vivendi, which already controls Telecom Italia, of violating Italian law. Said law prohibits the same company from exceeding certain thresholds for business turnover in the country. On 18 December 2019, the Advocate General of the European Union's Court of Justice ruled in favor of Vivendi by considering the Italian Government's calculation of the thresholds as "disproportionate" (De Laubier, 2020). This law relating to media plurality, invoked by the plaintiff in the complaint, would prevent the French company from maintaining its 28.8% stake in Mediaset. Although Italian law considered that Vivendi could not own both significant stakes in the incumbent operator Telecom Italia (of which it holds 24%) and Mediaset at the same time, in September 2020, the European Court of Justice "ruled that 'a restriction on the freedom of establishment may be justified by an objective of general interest', such as the protection of information and media pluralism. But that was 'not the case with the provision in question'" (Manière, 2020a).

Vivendi Regains Control of Havas

In May 2017, Vivendi announced its intention to acquire the Bolloré group's shares in Havas, i.e. 60% of the capital, for €2.36 billion (Rosemain & Barzic, 2017), before then launching a takeover bid to acquire 100% of the shares in that company. Havas, it is worth recalling, is a major French and international player in advertising, the sixth largest in the world, and one of Vivendi's ancestors. This operation raised several concerns, however. First, it drew the attention of the French stock market supervisory authorities, the Autorité des Marchés Financiers (AMF). The purchase price was set at €9.25 per share, its highest ever price. However, shortly after this, Havas announced poor financial results. Therefore, the Bolloré family has been accused of a conflict of interest for

> having sold its Havas shares at the highest price while knowing very well the financial situation of the Havas Group, and therefore the future fall in share value. [While] the links between the two companies are numerous. The Bolloré Group held [at that time] 60% of the Havas Group's shares and 20% of Vivendi's shares. Vincent's son, Yannick Bolloré, sits on the board of Vivendi while being CEO of the Havas Group and vice-president of the Bolloré Group. Just below him in the hierarchy of Havas is Dominique Delport, who also sits on the board of Vivendi.
> (Baudino, 2017)

Second, the operation between Havas, the Bolloré Group and Vivendi is characteristic of a practice that Vincent Bolloré has employed on several occasions, forcing Vivendi to buy assets from its own group, the Bolloré group. The cash earned by the Bolloré Group through the sale can then be reinvested in Vivendi's capital. It is largely thanks to this type of practice that Vincent Bolloré has succeeded in financing the gradual rise of his holding within Vivendi's capital.

Vivendi Regains a Foothold in Video Games

In October 2015, Vivendi acquired a 10.39% stake in Ubisoft, the third-largest publisher of video games in the world at the time (Manière, 2016), and a 10.2% stake in Gameloft (a publisher of games for smartphones). In February 2016, it launched a hostile takeover bid for the latter, taking over full control in July 2016. Founded by the Guillemot family, who also founded Ubisoft, Gameloft was only partially (20%) owned by the five Guillemot brothers (ibid.), and was a much smaller company than Ubisoft, with a turnover of €285 million in 2015 (Hélie, 2016). Vivendi's takeover resulted in Gameloft being valued at €700 million, much higher than its actual value according to many analysts. Ubisoft, on the other hand, had a market valuation of over €3.6 billion at the end of May 2016. During this period, Vivendi sold its stakes in other video game companies (Manière, 2016). In January 2016, the remaining stake in Activision Blizzard was sold for approximately 1 billion euros. However, a subsequent takeover bid for Ubisoft then failed, and in March 2018 Vivendi sold its 27.3% stake in the company for approximately €2 billion. The founding Guillemot family had always opposed the takeover, but above all, the Ubisoft share price tripled during the takeover bid, making the operation too expensive. This withdrawal from Ubisoft generated a significant capital gain of €1.2 billion for Vivendi (Manière, 2018d).

Vivendi Relaunches Its Book Publishing Activities

In July 2018, Vivendi announced its intention to acquire Editis from the Spanish company Grupo Planeta. For the most part, Editis is made up of the publishing houses that formerly belonged to Vivendi Universal Publishing (VUP). In 2017, it was the second-largest French publisher behind Hachette, owned by Lagardère, and ahead of Madrigall. The purchase price, €900 million, was deemed high due to the fact that Editis was in significant debt, valued at more than €1.2 billion. Although Editis owns around 50 publishing houses, some of which are very important in their field in France, such as Nathan, Robert Laffont, Plon, Pocket, 10/18, Bordas and even Le Cherche Midi, the company was struggling at that time. It had a difficult year in 2017, with a 7% drop in turnover (€759 million) and an operating profit of just €60 million (Vulser, 2018). The transaction was finalized in January 2019 and constituted the largest in book publishing in France since the financial group Wendel sold Editis to Planeta for 1 billion euros in 2008. Another major operation carried out in book publishing in France was the purchase of Flammarion by Gallimard for €251 million in 2012, the new group – the Madrigall group – assuming third position in the market (Debouté, 2019).

The Company Again Acquires Assets in Telecommunications

Vivendi acquired a 14.9% stake in Telecom Italia in June 2015, gradually increasing this to 23.8% by 1 March 2016 (La Tribune, 2016). "The French company was therefore barely below the 25% threshold synonymous with a public takeover bid according to Italian law" (ibid.). In this operation, Vivendi presented itself as an "industrial and non-financial investor" and a player "committed to the long term" (ibid.). However, beyond this statement relating to financial communication, many experts have considered Telecom Italia a very interesting target for raiders, insofar as its capital structure was very open at that time (the capital being diluted among many holders). Furthermore, at the time of the operation, the Italian telecommunications market was attractive and showed great potential, in particular because Internet networks and infrastructure were underdeveloped, especially broadband and fiber networks. Moreover, other French industrialists were interested in Telecom Italia. In October 2015, the French telecommunications operator, Iliad (Free), announced that it had acquired a potential 15.14% stake in Telecom Italia, although it has since withdrawn from the capital of the incumbent Italian telecommunications operator after opting for other forms of investment in the Italian telecommunications market (Dow Jones, 2016).

Ultimately, Vivendi was not able to launch a takeover bid for Telecom Italia or even maintain control over the operator's board of directors. Indeed, an American investment fund, Elliott, with 9% of the capital, succeeded in superseding Vivendi in this respect. Elliott officials "have repeatedly criticized Vivendi's 'mismanagement', while the French company believes that Elliott's only goal was "to 'dismantle' the operator to meet short-term objectives" (Manière, 2018b). Vivendi's fear was that under Elliot's influence, network activities would be spun-off, leaving Telecom Italia with only service provision activities, which would obviously reduce the value and strategic interest of its participation in the company's capital. Indeed, Telecom Italia created a subsidiary by the name of NetCo, which took ownership of the fixed Internet network. Italian regulatory authorities have also requested clarification of the distinction between networks and services. Telecom Italia decided that NetCo will have its own board of directors and its own management. In a press release, Telecom Italia has specified that NetCo will guarantee fair access to its fixed Internet network to all operators. In other words, this means that Telecom Italia will not, *a priori*, be favored in any way whatsoever *vis-à-vis* its competitors.

(Manière, 2018c)

This decision came following tensions between Vivendi and the Italian authorities. In September 2017,

the Consob, the Italian financial markets authority, ruled that Vivendi *de facto* controlled Telecom Italia. But the operator and Vivendi contested this assertion, even though the latter admitted to exercising 'management and coordination' activities within the operator. The disagreement came in a context of conflictual relations between the French and Italian governments following the French state's decision to nationalize a major French shipyard in order to prevent an Italian company from taking control.

(Manière, 2018c)

In October 2017, the Italian state decided to use the special powers afforded to it when Italian sovereignty is threatened (La Tribune, 2017). In an interview with Repubblica TV in mid-October, the Italian Minister of Industry, Carlo Calenda, very explicitly requested a division between network activities and services within Telecom Italia: "'Yes, yes, [the fixed network] should be spun-off and quoted on the stock market […] so that the market can judge for itself'. He added that he saw no problem with Telecom Italia having foreign shareholders, but only on condition that they 'stop treating [them] as a colony'" (Manière, 2018c). In May 2018, at a general meeting, Elliott took control of the Telecom Italia board of directors by obtaining the ten director positions that remained to be filled. With only five seats, Vivendi lost the *de facto* control it had exercised over Telecom Italia. Elliott proposed the appointment of several independent figures from the Italian business community to the board of directors.

In 2019, after the announcement of poor financial results, tensions eased somewhat between the two main shareholders in Telecom Italia. The operator had a debt of €25 billion at the time and announced a colossal loss of €1.4 billion for the third quarter of 2018, against a profit of €437 million in the same quarter the previous year. "The significant tensions between shareholders had affected the evolution of the stock, which lost 30% of its value in one year, in addition to the daily operations of Telecom Italia" (Manière, 2019). Vivendi had already spent over €4 billion on Telecom Italia and did not want to lose its stake (Schmitt & Tosseri, 2019). In March 2019, a solution emerged thanks to a public financial institution, the Deposits and Loans Fund (CDP) (Cassa Depositi e Prestiti), which was already represented on Telecom Italia's board of directors. Holding 9.82% of the operator's capital, CDP was the second-largest shareholder and was already in a position of arbitration between the two rivals. CDP had invested heavily in Open Fiber, a fixed network, and proposed linking this network with Telecom Italia's network, Netco (ibid.). This solution gradually took hold. In September 2020, Telecom Italia agreed to create a single fiber optic network in Italy, where the deployment of fiber was still not very advanced. The idea was to build this network, given the name AccessCo, on the basis of a merger between the networks of the energy company Enel (OpenFiber) and FiberCop, which was itself to unite the networks of Telecom Italia and Fastweb. "Under the terms of the deal, Tim will own at least 50.1% of AccessCo, which includes 'a shared governance mechanism with CDP'" (AFP, 2020b). "CDP is set to play a central role in the operation because, thanks to this merger, CDP holds 50% of Open Fiber in 2020" (ibid.).

A Very Profitable Trip to the Capital of the FNAC Group

In April 2016, Vivendi acquired a 15% stake in the capital of FNAC, the leading French company that owns supermarkets specializing in the retail of cultural products and electronic materials. This operation took place at a time when FNAC was trying to buy Darty, a leading French player in the sale of household appliances. FNAC was forced to seek funding in order to pay cash for its takeover of Darty, and Vivendi provided this. Vivendi withdrew from the capital of FNAC in July 2018, realizing a capital gain of €108 million for an initial investment of €159 million (Letessier, 2018).

A Partial Sale of the Capital of Universal Music Group

In December 2019, Vivendi announced the signing of an agreement with a consortium led by Tencent for the sale of 10% of its stake in Universal Music Group. The exact composition of this consortium has remained a secret. The sale left Vivendi with €3 billion, UMG being valued at €30 billion. Tencent already had links with Vivendi, as Tencent Music was listed on the New York Stock Exchange in December 2018 and Vivendi was one of its shareholders. According to Vivendi's financial communication, Tencent's entry into the capital would allow UMG to increase its digital presence and revenues in a booming Chinese market and more broadly in Asian countries: "Vivendi is delighted at the arrival of Tencent and its co-investors, which will allow for greater development in the Asian market" (Capital, 2020). Vivendi also started negotiations for the possible sale of additional minority interests (L'Express Press Room & AFP, 2019).

> The consortium may acquire up to an additional 10% stake in UMG until January 15, 2021. This transaction is completed by means of a separate agreement allowing Tencent Music Entertainment to acquire a minority stake in the capital of the subsidiary of UMG regrouping its Chinese activities.
>
> (Capital, 2020)

In addition, Vivendi announced that it will sell "various additional minority stakes in UMG with the assistance of several banks. An IPO is scheduled for early 2023 at the latest" (ibid.). In July 2019, Vivendi had announced its intention to sell up to 50% of Universal Music Group capital, taking advantage of the publication of very good half-year results, with an increase of over 18%, to make its announcement. Vivendi also said it was looking for "one or more strategic partners" (AFP & Reuters, 2019).

The Takeover Bid for Lagardère

In April 2020, Vivendi began to acquire a stake in Lagardère. When announcing the acquisition of a 10.6% stake, it specified that this constituted a "long-term financial investment" (AFP, 2020c). Lagardère has its origins in a former French company, Matra, which was active in the aerospace and automotive industries. This group led by Jean-Luc Lagardère, the father of the company's CEO, Arnaud Lagardère, had its heyday in French capitalism from the 1960s to the 1970s and was notably dependent on orders from the French state. From the 1980s onwards, Matra diversified into communication and media and became transnational in size. The company was at one stage the world leader in magazine publishing and was also active in pay television and advertising-funded television, book publishing, print, radio, multimedia, etc. Following Jean-Luc Lagardère's death in 2003, Arnaud succeeded him. Since that point, the company has focused more on the media and cultural industries, assets outside these areas gradually having been sold off. However, Lagardère has experienced very significant difficulties in recent years, recording poor operating results. To cope with its expenses and pay dividends to its shareholders, the company has been forced to continually sell assets, including almost all activities related to the magazine press, even its flagship in women's publishing, the magazine *Elle*. In 2020, following these disposals, Lagardère still remains a major player in media and entertainment in France. The company is active in book publishing through Hachette (the biggest French book publishing company) and also in retail via Lagardère Travel Retail. It also owns influential French media: the radio station Europe1 and the newspapers *Paris Match* and *Le Journal du Dimanche*. Lagardère enjoys a special legal status: it is called a "limited partnership by share" *(société en commandite par action)*. With this type of company, management is entrusted to a holding company owned by the Lagardère family via legal statutes, which make it possible to control the company with only a small share of the capital. However, its poor financial results made Lagardère an ideal target for raiders such as Vincent Bolloré, via Vivendi, as well as for the investment fund, Amber Capital. Indeed, the Vivendi takeover bid was carried out in consultation with the aforementioned investment fund, which already had a stake in Lagardère and was challenging Arnaud Lagardère's management of the company. Prior to the takeover, Amber held a little over 16% of Lagardère's capital and 12% of the voting rights. But the fund had called for the departure of Arnaud Lagardère and the almost entire renewal of the company's supervisory board (AFP, 2020c). The other major shareholders in Lagardère were the sovereign fund of Qatar, which held 13% of the shares and 20% of the voting rights, and Arnaud Lagardère himself, with a little more than 7% of the shares and 10% of the voting rights (ibid.). Vivendi launched its takeover bid after the sale of 10% of the capital of UMG.

In July 2020, Vivendi became the largest shareholder in Lagardère with 21.19% of its capital, changing its strategy with regard to management of the company. After stating that it did not plan to "exert influence on the strategic choices" made by Lagardère, Vivendi's management then said it was considering applying for a place on the supervisory board (Manière, 2020b), a change in direction that was linked to intervention by Bernard Arnault. In fact, in May 2020, Arnault's holding company, Groupe Arnault, had acquired a 25% stake in Lagardère Capital & Management (LCM), Arnaud Lagardère's holding company, which was in charge of managing

Lagardère. As mentioned earlier, this control was exerted despite only having a little over 7% of the company's capital, due to the special status afforded Lagardère. Bernard Arnault is the owner of LVMH and one of the richest men in the world, and Vivendi justified its change of attitude toward Lagardère's management as the result of the new situation created by Bernard Arnault's entry into the capital of the Lagardère family holding company, which would generate uncertainties "concerning the decision-making processes within Lagardère" (ibid.). This entry into LCM capital was linked to the holding company's very precarious financial situation. Indeed, according to Arnaud Lagardère's statements to AFP and Le Point (a French newspaper), it had debts amounting to €164 million in 2019. As a result, given Lagardère's stock market valuation at the time, LCM's stake in Lagardère was only worth €106 million. In other words, the holding company was in a situation of virtual bankruptcy, something Arnaud Lagardère himself confirmed recently. However, in a partnership limited by shares (*société en commandite par actions*), the general partner is indefinitely liable for the debts of the company through his own personal assets. From this perspective, Arnaud Lagardère's participation in his group served as a guarantee for the repayment of debts contracted by his holding company. Groupe Arnault's acquisition of a stake was therefore essential to safeguard LCM (Manière, 2020c). In fact, at a general meeting of shareholders in May 2020, Amber Capital announced its intention to take control of the supervisory board and change the statutes of Lagardère to prevent it from remaining a limited partnership with shares.

Various important figures showed their support for Arnaud Lagardère, including Nicolas Sarkozy, the former President of the French Republic, and Guillaume Pepy, the former chairman of SNCF (the historic French railway company). This impacted the choice made by the sovereign investment fund, the Qatar Investment Authority, the group's second largest shareholder with a 13% stake, to also lend its support to Arnaud Lagardère (ibid.). In September 2020, Bernard Arnault increased his presence within Lagardère. In addition to spending around €80 million within Arnaud Lagardère's financial holding, he acquired a 5.5% stake in Lagardère, paid at market price, i.e. around 100 million euros (AFP, 2020a). Arnault also obtained one of the four seats on the board of directors of Arjil Commanditée – Arco, one of the companies with the power to manage Lagardère.

Many experts consider that Vincent Bolloré plans to acquire certain assets of Lagardère, and especially the international activities of Hachette, which Vivendi could bring into Editis. Arnaud

Lagardère has stated that he will personally oppose "any dismantling of [his] group" (Manière, 2020d). In August 2020, Vivendi and Amber Capital, which had become the two largest shareholders in Lagerdère, entered into a pact concerning the company's governance in order to obtain seats on its supervisory board (Reuters, 2020). In September 2020, following the announcement of the rise of Bernard Arnault within Lagardère, Vivendi and the Amber Capital fund filed a legal action to hold an exceptional general meeting and obtain the appointment of four members to the supervisory board. Between them, the two owned 45% of Lagardère's capital. The request was considered legitimate by the Qatari sovereign wealth fund (AFP, 2020a).

What Can We Conclude from the Outcome of All These Operations?

Since the arrival of Vincent Bolloré, his financial group and his family to Vivendi, the company has engaged in numerous acquisition operations. Three observations can be drawn from the analysis of these transactions. First, in accordance with the history of Vivendi but also the practices of Vincent Bolloré, these operations pursue both industrial and financial objectives. Beyond the financial communication discourse that emphasizes the industrial issues of these acquisitions, it is often difficult to discern the industrial aims from the financial ones. An acquisition that may initially have an industrial objective may later turn out to be of purely financial interest. The opposite argument can also be made, a financial transaction, such as Vivendi's rise in Lagardère's capital, may have industrial interests, such as seizing part of Lagardère's book publishing assets.

Second, a further characteristic of these recent operations also clearly emerges. These strategies belong to the capitalist sphere, directly involving private interests, and especially those of Vincent Bolloré. But these operations also raise important political issues, which may be issues of public policy but are frequently associated with more political or even international political issues. In this regard, the operations carried out in Italy were at the heart of the tensions that arose between France and Italy on various industrial matters.

Third, these diversification strategies are risky and not all of them have been successful. Vivendi is caught up in permanent games surrounding disposals and acquisitions, largely linked to chance opportunities, and subject to many unforeseeable and uncontrollable risks, without any strategic industrial vision emerging from this series of operations. The success or failure of such strategies depends, in addition to political issues, on the reactions of other major industrial or financial players, as illustrated by Bernard Arnault's entry into Lagardère's capital, thwarting the plans of Vivendi and Vincent Bolloré. Certain operations can therefore turn out to be both dangerous and very risky. For example, the takeover bids for Mediaset and Telecom Italia have stalled. Vivendi has spent large sums on these, while the advantages, both industrial and financial, are slow to appear. The diversity of Vivendi's positioning plays an important role in this regard. It is essential for the company to have stable resources derived from subsidiaries whose industrial activity is profitable or even flourishing, and that report a significant EBITA. This assures Vivendi of maintaining a correct net income and of having the resources to distribute significant dividends to its shareholders. The links between speculative financial stocks and in particular the various takeover bids on the one hand and the presence of long-term and remunerative industrial activities on the other are therefore subtle. Whatever the issues raised by these diversification strategies, their importance is such that Vivendi's industrial positioning since the arrival of Vincent Bolloré has profoundly changed. It is now once more a conglomerate with very diversified activities, as in the days of Vivendi Universal, though to a lesser extent. We shall now review the operation of the various subsidiaries that make up Vivendi and issues associated with this.

Vivendi, a Conglomerate of Business Activities with Few Synergies and Very Different Dynamics

While before Vincent Bolloré's arrival and after the sale of assets in telecommunications Vivendi's activities focused on recorded music through UMG on a transnational scale, and on pay television, especially in France, in just a few years, the structure of the company has completely evolved to now include advertising activities, through Havas, and book publishing, through Editis. These latter two segments formed part of what was formerly Vivendi Universal. In addition, Vivendi now also owns some gaming businesses via Gameloft (Vivendi Universal was also positioned in video games, but via other subsidiaries). In addition to these large segments, the company has also branched out into various activities related to the performing arts, grouped together under Vivendi Village. The company also holds significant stakes in Telecom Italia, Mediaset and the Banijay Group, the world leader in television production. Table 3.1 provides an overview of Vivendi's activities and subsidiaries.

Table 3.2 that follows illustrates how Vivendi's sales are broken down.

Table 3.1 Structure of Vivendi as of December 31, 2019

Universal Music Group (100%)	Groupe Canal+ (100%)	Havas Group (100%)	Editis (100%)	Gameloft (100%)	Vivendi Village (100%)	Nouvelles initiatives (New initiatives) (100%)	Participations
Recorded Music (UMG)	France Pole (Canal+)	Havas Creative Group	Literature	Gameloft SE (France)	Talent (talent agent)	Dailymotion	Telecom Italia (23.94%)
Musical edition (UMPG)	International Division Canal+ International	Havas Media Group	Educational and reference books	Gameloft Inc. (United States)	Live	GVA (Group Vivendi Africa)	Mediaset (28.80%)
Merchandising Bravado	Cinema Division Studiocanal	Havas Health & You	Distribution and marketing	Gameloft Inc. Divertissement (Canada) Gameloft Software Beijing (China)	Performance halls Ticketing		Banijay Group Holding (31.40%)

Table created by the author based on data from the 2019 annual report (6–7).

Table 3.2 Revenue and EBITA (earnings before interest, taxes and amortization) of the main components of Vivendi in 2019 and 2018

	UMG	Groupe Canal+	Havas	Editis	Gameloft	Vivendi Village	Nouvelles initiatives	Elimination of operations between company subsidiaries
Revenue 2019	€7,1559 million	€5,268 million	€2,378 million	€687 million	€259	€141 million	€71 million	€65 million
Revenue 2018	€6,023 million	€5,166 million	€2,319 million	/	€293	€123 million	€66 million	€58 million
EBITA 2019	€1,124 million	€343 million	€225 million	€52 million	€36 million	€17 million	€65 million	€100 million
EBITA 2018	€902 million	€400 million	€215 million	/	€2 million	€9 million	€99 million	€123 million

Table created by the author based on data from Vivendi's annual report 2019 (205).

Table 3.2 shows the impact that the two historical activities of Vivendi, UMG and the Canal+ Group, have on the company's financial results. Together, in 2019 these two segments had a turnover of €12.427 billion, or 78.16% of the company's total revenue, and an EBITA of €1.467 million, or 96.13% of Vivendi's EBITA. UMG plays a very special role, since this subsidiary represents 45.03% of Vivendi's turnover and 73.65% of its EBITA. These two segments aside, only the Havas Group makes a significant contribution to Vivendi's financial results. In terms of turnover, and even more so in terms of EBITA, Vivendi's other activities are of little importance. Of course, the figures may hide some important facts. Does Vivendi want to combine activities with a low EBITA, such as book publishing, with other activities like audiovisual and recorded music because of the synergies that could develop between them? Or have the diversification operations carried out since 2016 mainly had financial objectives: taking advantage of an opportunity to acquire an external company at a lower price in order to then sell it on later with a significant capital gain?

According to Vivendi's financial communication, the objective would be to create an integrated company active in several media with transnational offers and whose various components present strong synergies. Entertainment is said to be Vivendi's "DNA": "The refocusing on content and media that took place in 2014 was a profitable choice for the group. Each new investment, each new project allows this strategy to take shape and unite the group around a common DNA: entertainment" (Vivendi, 2019: 12). Yannick Bolloré, one of Vincent Bolloré's sons and chairman of the supervisory board, has declared:

> Vivendi is also an industrial project, which is based on one lever: integration. The great strength of our group is to multiply the bridges between our different businesses. When the music of Universal Music Group (UMG) accompanies an Editis literary release, or when Havas supports the communication of Canal+, we make our entities grow together. Many joint projects emerged in 2019, which we will continue to develop.
> (Vivendi, 2019: 4)

Again according to Vivendi's financial communication, three elements would form the basis of these synergies. The first common point in most of Vivendi's businesses is talent management:

> Throughout the content value chain, which revolves around talent, live and audiovisual production, theaters, merchandising...

> Vivendi has a unique ecosystem capable of offering tailor-made services with the collaboration of several entities, which enable it to promote all talents, internal and external.
>
> (Vivendi, 2019: 13)

Technology constitutes the second bridge linking the various activities of the company:

> Beyond content issues, all Vivendi entities work together on technical and technological subjects, enabling them to accelerate the development of each business by imagining the group of the future. From 5G to artificial intelligence via blockchain, the group is working on cross-functional projects that will allow it to better meet the needs of the content consumers of tomorrow. In addition, Vivendi has entered into partnerships with major international players in tech and media.
>
> (Vivendi, 2019: 13)

The third link is the ambition to be an international player: "Being among the world leaders in media, content and communication means developing in several sectors" (Vivendi, 2019: 15). In respect of this, Yannick Bolloré has stated: "Vivendi's ambition is to be one of the world leaders in culture, at the crossroads of entertainment, media and communication. We are already number one in Europe and are growing year by year" (Vivendi, 2019: 4). The "new territories" (new for Vivendi) of Asia and Africa offer unique prospects for an integrated company like Vivendi:

> The integrated industrial company formed today by Vivendi is also increasing its opportunities in fast-growing regions: Africa and Asia. The entertainment industries are growing very rapidly there. The music market, for example, is growing exponentially in China; in Africa, the smartphone boom is causing significant demand for content; new uses are appearing with connected speakers, etc. Vivendi thus intends to offer an alternative to the major American and Asian players in markets where diversity of content is key.
>
> (Vivendi, 2019: 13)

Taken as a whole, given that it is active in 81 countries, Vivendi has a *de facto* transnational dimension:

> In 2019, around 54% of its sales were generated in Europe, where it is established in 22 countries, 32% in the Americas,

10% in Asia-Oceania and 4% in Africa. Since 7 January 2020, Vivendi has been registered in the form of a European company, the transition to this new status making it possible to align its social form with its European roots.

(Vivendi, 2019: 15)

Various examples of transversal operations are cited to illustrate the synergies that exist between the various components of the company:

> UMG working with Editis, the Canal+ Group, the Havas Group, is now a reality. Many projects have been carried out jointly by several businesses: the after show of Bigflo and Oli after the Top 14 final at the Stade de France, the Harlan Coben party at the Olympia or the organization of the Canaltour in Douala (Cameroon). The multiplication of these collaborations allows the company to have the flexibility and necessary resources to explore new formats; the creation of Vivendi Brand Marketing, a structure combining in-depth knowledge of consumers and the brands owned by the Havas Group with know-how in creativity, production and distribution of Vivendi's other activities. It provides brand content strategy advice to brands around the world; internal work on themes common to all entities.
>
> (Vivendi, 2019: 13)

These examples are only fairly minor or even anecdotal cross-sectorial operations. Thus, it is necessary to examine the industrial dynamics that underlie them, subsidiary by subsidiary. To this end, it will be possible to assess the extent to which these different subsidiaries and activities present synergies with one another or whether these activities are completely compartmentalized, each with their own specific industrial logics.

Universal Music Group

UMG is the group's primary asset and has a presence in nearly 60 countries. In 2019, UMG achieved a turnover of €7,159 million (45% of Vivendi's turnover) and an EBITA of €1,124 million (Vivendi, 2019: 15). The world's largest recorded music company, UMG hires 8,865 of Vivendi's 44,641 employees. It is active in all musical fields, as indicated by its main labels: Capitol Music Group, Republic Records, Interscope Geffen A&M Records, Island Records, Def Jam Recordings, Universal Music Group Nashville, Universal Music

Latin Entertainment, Polydor, Blue Note Records, Decca, Deutsche Grammophon, and Verve, among others. The company has artists of great note under contract, including The Beatles, The Rolling Stones, U2, Andrea Bocelli, Lady Gaga, Taylor Swift, Queen, Helene Fischer, and many others. It also has artists under contract who had very good record sales or very good listening results on streaming platforms in 2019, including Billie Eilish, Post Malone, Ariana Grande, J. Balvin, Halsey, Lewis Capaldi and Shawn Mendes. In other words, UMG's position allows it to have both catalog artists (whose songs sell over a long period of time) and emerging artists. The company has three main activities: recorded music, music publishing and merchandising.

The recorded music business represents almost 80% of UMG's consolidated sales. This activity has of course been greatly affected since the 2000s by various movements linked to the deployment of Internet, including illegal downloads and players from the communication industries[1] entering the music economy, especially in relation to music distribution. These phenomena generated both a drop in record sales and in margins. For example, the creation of iTunes by Apple in the early 2000s led to lower prices for recorded music. By selling individual tracks for 99 cents, iTunes determined a benchmark price. Although the rise of streaming platforms has brought a clear improvement in financial results, they have not returned to the levels of the early 2000s. It is worth noting that the major players in recorded music, and especially UMG, have entered into very profitable agreements with these platforms. The company has become involved in streaming on a mass scale:

> UMG has signed licensing agreements with more than 400 platforms around the world. In 2019, UMG's revenue from subscriptions and streaming represented 59% of recorded music revenue. The licensed streaming platforms generate recurring revenue and provide statistical data. The streaming model has increased the importance of owning a catalog of titles. This is an asset for UMG, which has one of the largest catalogs of recorded music in the world.
>
> (Vivendi, 2019: 15)

Universal Music Publishing Group (UMPG) is the music publishing subsidiary of UMG and licenses the use of titles for sound recordings, films, television shows, commercials, and video games, as well as for live and public performances. It also grants licenses for compositions used in sheet music and song portfolios. Usually, UMPG licenses a title after acquiring an interest in its copyright and entering into an agreement with the artist. It owns and controls an extensive catalog of original music and arrangements (Vivendi, 2019: 15).

UMG's merchandising and marketing subsidiary is called Bravado. It connects artists (beginners and experienced) with recent or long-established brands, offering them comprehensive campaigns including product creation, partnerships and promotion. The products created are sold through in-store and online retailers, specialty stores, on concert tours and in limited edition retail sales. Bravado also grants licensing rights to numerous third-party companies around the world (Vivendi, 2019: 15).

In terms of synergies with the rest of the company, the links between UMG and audiovisual activities are highlighted in Vivendi's financial communication:

> Cinema releases also contribute to UMG's performance: the soundtracks of the A Star is Born films (2018), by Lady Gaga and Bradley Cooper, Bohemian Rhapsody (2018), inspired by the titles of Queen, and Joker (2019), by composer Hildur Guðnadóttir, have met with great success.
> (Vivendi, 2019: 12)

However, it is thanks to the boom in streaming and contracts with big stars, that is to say, to a dynamic specific to recorded music, that Vivendi has been able to increase its turnover: "UMG confirms its success with a record year 2019. Its turnover amounted to €7.2 billion, up 14% (at constant scope and exchange rates) compared to 2018. This strong growth is still largely driven by streaming, which continues to grow" (Vivendi, 2019: 12).

The Canal+ Group

In 2019, the Canal+ Group achieved sales of €5,268 million euros (33.1% of Vivendi's sales) and an EBITA of €343 million. It has 7,826 employees and is present in 40 countries. The company has three main activities: pay and free television in France, international television and cinema. Pay and free television in France represents 58% of the group's turnover, international pay television 34% and

StudioCanal (cinema) for 8% (Vivendi, 2019: 15). Its subsidiary StudioCanal aside, the Canal+ Group derives most of its turnover from monthly subscriptions: it has 20.3 million subscribers, 8.4 million of whom are in France. Subscriptions are marketed directly on all distribution networks (Internet, satellite, TNT) and through partnerships with Internet service providers (3.4 million customers at the end of 2019). French television therefore comprises the main activity of the Canal+ Group, although international television is its most dynamic segment. An analysis of the distribution of turnover within the group and its evolution from 2017 to 2020 shows that although television activities in France have been dominant, the turnover in both this segment and the film production segment (StudioCanal) is declining. Only international television activities are growing. It is the dynamism of this international television segment that explains the overall increase in the Canal+ Group's turnover. However, this increase is mainly explained by an increase in the segment's scope, with television companies having been acquired overseas as shown in the Table 3.3 below.

In France, the Canal+ Group offers a premium general-interest channel, Canal+, which broadcasts films, series and sports in particular, with five specialized channels (Cinema, Sport, Family, Décalé and Séries). In addition, the Canal+ Group's products also include around 20 company-owned thematic channels and 130 French and international external channels. The group is also active in the free television market in France via its three national channels (C8, CNews and CStar). The main source of income for these three television channels is advertising. Canal Brand Solutions is in charge of marketing advertising on those channels, as well as that

Table 3.3 Breakdown and change in revenue for the three Canal Group segments (2019–2017)

Revenue (in millions of euros)	2019	2018	2017
Television in mainland France	3,053	3,137	3,249
Television abroad and in French overseas territories	1,781	1,567	1,482
Studiocanal	434	462	467
Total	5,268	5,166	5,198

Table created by the author based on data published in Vivendi's 2019 and 2018 reports (Vivendi 2018: 208, 2019: 202).

of some 15 thematic channels. The Canal+ Group therefore has a very rich array of products on offer in France. Since the creation of the Canal+ channel in 1984, pay television in France has essentially consisted of linear television channels. Prices have remained high and consumers have had little alternative to the expensive option of Canal+. Thus, in 2020, Canal+ still mainly offers packages of linear TV channels and prices still tend to be high.

However, since the mid-2010s, the company has experienced significant difficulties in its television activities in France, especially in pay television. Various movements explain these difficulties. First, the Canal+ model that was built in 1984 now seems quite outdated. In recent years, the French pay-TV market has evolved enormously due to the arrival of new operators, and especially operators of Subscription Video on Demand (SVoD) platforms, like Netflix. New ways of viewing television have emerged, in particular with consumption on smartphones, catch-up television and on-demand. The entry of Netflix into the French market therefore brought with it important repercussions for Canal+. By focusing on a non-linear offer, at low prices compared with Canal+, and comprising a lot of attractive American content (television series but also films), Netflix found immediate and massive success.

Second, at the same time as the arrival of Netflix, Canal+ lost the monopoly on its broadcasting of major soccer matches. Two companies have acquired these broadcasting rights: BeIn Sports, a Qatari company, and Mediapro, a Spanish audiovisual group, whose shareholders are predominantly Chinese and British. These two companies specializing in sports have raised the stakes for the acquisition of broadcasting rights to a level too high for a more mainstream player like Canal+. In addition to sports content, Canal+ has also lost a significant portion of its content distribution contracts with American studios, since the decision of the major American players to develop their own SVoD subsidiaries in reaction to the success of Netflix has had a great impact. These major Hollywood studios have gradually decided to restrict sales of broadcasting rights for their content to foreign players, preferring to reserve these for their own SVod subsidiaries, who offer it on a transnational scale. Canal+ has thus partly lost its role as a relay for American television series and films, content that made a fairly large contribution to the success of Canal+ with French consumers. The loss of this content has therefore considerably reduced the attractiveness of Canal+ to potential subscribers.

Third, competition has also come from players whose core business is outside the audiovisual industry. Indeed, the deployment of SVoD platforms has led to an abundant supply of content, partly from "new entrants" to these markets. These are national players in the telecommunications industries (Orange and SFR) or transnational digital players, including Amazon. What these actors have in common is that they lower tariffs, because they consider the supply of cultural products to be less a direct source of income than a set of joint products that make it possible to distinguish their content from that of their competitors or to collect data on consumers, data that are necessary to better value their main product or service (connection services or e-commerce). As a result, they may accept losses on such content. Orange's expenses to ensure content exclusivity are very high, as are those of SFR with the major American studios (Discovery and NBCUniversal): $30 million per year for Orange with HBO alone. The full amount and duration of HBO's contract with Orange have not been released. At the time the contract was agreed, however, Orange was investing €550 million per year in content (Piquard, 2017). This is an enormous sum compared with the limited size of the French market and the competitive challenge for Canal+ is therefore a considerable one.

Due to the three aforementioned phenomena, Canal+, which enjoyed a *de facto* near-monopoly in the pay-TV market or, at least, a very strong dominant position in France for around 30 years, suddenly lost subscribers and revenue. The decline in subscribers began before Netflix entered the French market, however. "In mainland France, the group has suffered 12 years of decline in subscribers. In total, it lost nearly 2 million followers over this period, to 4.5 million subscribers in the fourth quarter of 2019" (Manière, 2020e). In particular, there has been a fall in the number of individual subscribers in metropolitan France with self-distribution, from 4.950 million in 2017, to 4.733 million in 2018 and then 4.548 million in 2019 (Vivendi 2018: 208, 2019: 202). Canal+ customers stemming from partnerships with telecoms operators have declined slightly over the past three years: from 3.17 million in 2017, to 3.093 million in 2018 and then 3 million in 2019 (Vivendi 2018: 208, 2019: 202). In total, the Canal+ Group had 8.4 million subscribers in mainland France as of 31 December 2019, which is the largest customer base for a pay-TV company in France (Vivendi 2019: 27).

This decrease in the number of subscribers up until 2020, and especially those who subscribe directly with Canal+ rather than through other channels, has led to a drop in revenues and even losses in some years. By way of example, Canal+ France suffered an operating loss of €399 million in 2016. These difficulties, which, as mentioned, began before Netflix entered the French market in 2014, continued in 2019:

> Television revenues in mainland France fell slightly (–2.8% at constant scope and exchange rate) due to the decline in the portfolio of self-distributed individual subscribers. On the other hand, the Canal+ subscriber portfolio has recorded a net growth of 72,000 subscribers over the last 12 months.
> (Vivendi, 2019: 203)

Moreover, in 2018, "Canal+ was forced to make savings of €460 million over three years" (Manière, 2020e). Thus, the Canal+ Group's entire model, and especially the range of linear television channel packages, has proven to be quite outdated.

Faced with these changes and challenges, Canal+ has developed various strategies. The structure of the content and prices has been revised to make these more modular and more flexible (without subscription or with a 12- or 24-month subscription). Likewise, Canal+ has developed an SVoD product. This is not completely new, however, since it has offered SVod services under the Canal Play brand since 2011. However, the content offered via Canal Play was of lesser interest so as to not compete with Canal+'s main content, which was much more profitable for the company. In addition, the "Autorité de la concurrence" (the independent French authority in charge of regulating competition) had long prohibited Canal Play from offering exclusive content. Facing head-on competition with the arrival of Netflix, subscriber numbers fell "from 800,000 to 200,000" between 2014 and 2018 (Manière, 2018a). In 2019, a new and more attractive product has replaced Canal Play. Going by the name of SVoD Canal+ Séries, it includes better content, especially in terms of television series, and is offered at the relatively low price for the French market of €6.99.

More fundamentally, the Canal+ Group has chosen to drastically reorientate its activities to become an aggregator. Previously, Canal+ had a policy of vertical integration, meaning that it sought to control the entire production chain from producing content to selling subscriptions. The monetization of Canal+ was focused on mastering the whole value chain. Since 2016, the company has become a distributor of services, its own but also those of others companies. Thus, Canal+ has entered into distribution agreements with companies that were, and still are in 2020, its main competitors, including RMC Sport, beIN Sports, Netflix and Disney. Likewise, "in December 2019, the Canal+ Group announced the conclusion of an agreement with The Walt Disney Company France. Vivendi obtained exclusive distribution of the Disney group's channels and services, the first window to broadcast Disney films and associated studios (including Pixar, Marvel, Lucas Films, 20th Century Fox), and also became the exclusive distributor of the new service of Disney+ streaming in France" (Vivendi, 2019: 27). The Canal + Group also entered into an exclusive distribution agreement for beIN Sports channels from 1 June 2020. Under the terms of this agreement, Canal+ also obtained the exclusive sub-license for the 2020–2024 Ligue 1 soccer rights held by beIN Sports, allowing it to broadcast two matches per day, including 28 of the 38 best Ligue 1 games of each season (Vivendi, 2019: 27). Canal+'s strategy is to "become the privileged gateway to access other media players, such as OCS, the package of pay-TV channels from Orange, BeIN Sports, RMC Sport, Netflix, and the new Disney+ video on demand" (Manière, 2020e). In return, Canal+ accepted that its own services be marketed by other players. These include telecommunications operators such as Orange, or SVoD players such as Netflix, for example. In just a few months, the partnerships concluded with the telecom operators Orange and Free (Iliad) in the fall of 2016 resulted in more than 2.9 million new subscription contracts to Canal+ services via offers made by these two telecommunications operators. In short, the development of such an aggregation function allows players to organize competition within a context where there is an abundance of offers and consumers are starting to take out several subscriptions. Players thus rely on various competitive advantages linked to their core business: their mastery of networks and Internet access boxes, their number of subscribers or the quality of their content (Les Echos, 2017).

Furthermore, Canal+ decided to take back control of the soccer broadcasting it had previously lost, obtaining these broadcasting rights either exclusively or in association with BeIn Sports. This policy cost several hundred million euros, but was considered essential by the management of the company to keep up with competing offers. New television series have also been put into production. Thus, Canal+ is jointly developing two strategies: one of distributing content from other players and another of continuing to improve its own content in order to increase its attractiveness to current subscribers or potential subscribers.

The pay-TV segment has seen significant international growth in recent times. "International revenue increased strongly by 13.7% (+ 6.1% at constant scope and exchange rates) driven by both organic growth and the integration of M7" (Vivendi, 2019: 203). This segment had 11.9 million subscribers at the end of 2019. In a very important operation in May 2019, the Canal+ Group acquired M7 from an investment fund for a sum of around 1 billion euros, paid in cash.

> The Canal+ Group hopes to approach 20 million subscribers worldwide thanks to this pay TV operator (3 million subscribers), based in Luxembourg, which distributes channels such as Disney Channel, HBO, Eurosport and National Geographic in the Benelux and in Central Europe [...] M7 aggregates and distributes local and international channels, via satellite and OTT platforms (online services), in Belgium, the Netherlands, Austria, the Czech Republic, Slovakia, Hungary and Romania.
> (AFP, 2019)

According to Maaxime Saada, this is

> the biggest acquisition of Canal+ since the takeover of its competitor TPS [in 2005]. Except that at the time, it was a defensive move to make a competitor disappear [...]. Here, it is an offensive movement to establish itself in new territories.
> (AFP & Le Monde, 2019)

The operation helped to rapidly increase the number of Canal+ Group subscribers outside France:

> At the end of March, [the Canal+ Group] had a total of 15.7 million customers, a little over 7 million of these abroad. Prior to this point, it had mostly been Africa that dominated, with 4 million subscribers. 'We are going to increase to almost 20 million customers, which is almost a doubling of our subscriber base since the arrival of Vincent Bolloré in 2015", Maxime Saada said'.
> (Ibid.)

It is also expected to have a positive impact on the Canal+ Group's financial results: "M7, which generates a turnover of €400 million and 'operational profitability of 20%', according to Jacques du Puy, president of Canal+ International, has a higher profitability rate than that of the Canal+ group" (ibid.). M7's profits were around 8% in 2018 (ibid.). Another reason for this operation was to prevent competitors from getting their hands on M7:

> Canal+ would have concluded this takeover even before it was put on the market by Astorg, thanks to the good relations of the financial director Grégoire Castaing with the fund of investment. 'Comcast, telecom operators and others were eyeing the company. So there was an issue of speed', du Puy noted.
>
> (Ibid.)

Finally, the challenge also lies in creating synergies with the other activities of the Canal+ Group: "One of the objectives of the acquisition of M7, which is a content aggregation platform, is for the Canal+ group to distribute its own content more widely (to M7 subscribers) and so to better amortize their production costs" (ibid.). A further aim is to offer the non-linear television services of the Canal+ Group, and in particular MyCanal, in countries where M7 is established. This logic of economies of scale is particularly important in activities that have a significant proportion of fixed costs, such as content production or the implementation of a digital platform. However, it is debatable whether the Canal+ Group is engaged in transnationalization here (with joint and transnational offers), or rather this is merely a juxtaposition of different positions in national markets with specific content on offer. On the other hand, through the acquisition of M7, the Canal+ Group confirmed the strategic orientation it took in 2016, namely to move toward aggregator functions.

The Canal+ Group is also a producer and distributor of motion pictures and TV series through its subsidiary Studiocanal. It produces / co-produces or distributes around 50 films per year. This production activity is a legacy of the group's history. When the private pay channel Canal+ was created in 1984, the plan was for it to be the financier of French cinema in return for the advantages and protections the company has benefited from since its creation. For example, as noted in the chapter on the company's history, for a long time the public authorities have done everything possible to ensure that Canal+ is the only authorized terrestrial pay television channel in France. In addition to the above, some of the exclusive content offered by the Canal+ Group is produced by StudioCanal, which has a film catalog of over 6,000 titles. However,

StudioCanal's contribution to the Canal+ Group's financial results is limited. "Studiocanal's turnover was €434 million, down on 2018 (−12.8% at constant scope and exchange rates) due to the release of fewer films" (Vivendi, 2019: 203).

In short, the industrial dynamics that the Canal+ Group is involved in seem to be very specific and without any significant links to the other activities of the company.

The Havas Group

The Havas Group is one of the world's six largest players in the advertising industry. The company has three operational units: advertising creation, media, and health and "well-being". Havas Creative is the entity dedicated to creation and the backbone of the group's activity. According to Vivendi's financial communication, it brings together all fields of communication expertise to offer brands tailor-made solutions. It includes the global network comprising Havas Creative, Havas Edge, BETC Group, AMO and Arnold. Havas Media is focused on purchasing media and advertising space, and comprises two main brands: Havas Media and Arena Media. Present in more than 144 countries, Havas Media offers advertising space purchasing, mobile, data, performance marketing, advertising, and social media services. Havas Health & You brings together a network of health and well-being communication brands. Its main structures are Havas Life, Health4Brands (H4B), Havas Lynx, HVH and Havas PR, as well as dozens of other specialist agencies. It is the largest health communication network in the world (Vivendi, 2019: 33).

This Vivendi subsidiary has experienced difficulties in recent years due to changes in the advertising business and the growing role of some of the major players in the communication industries, including Google and Facebook. "The Havas Group's revenue was €2,378 million in 2019, up 2.6% (−1.0% at constant scope and exchange rates) compared to 2018" (Vivendi, 2019: 204). The financial results improved somewhat in 2019:

> Havas Group consolidates its profitability. Adjusted operating profit (EBITA) before restructuring charges amounted to € 260 million, up 6.1% compared to 2018. After restructuring charges, EBITA amounted to €225 million, a 4.5% growth. The EBITA/net income margin thus gained +0.2 points.
>
> (Vivendi, 2019: 204)

Although the group is clearly experiencing the same issues as other advertising agencies, on the occasion of the purchase of an American agency, Battery, which specializes in cultural content, Yannick Bolloré declared:

> The convergence of advertising, entertainment, music and games remains a priority for Havas and Vivendi, and Havas is an essential element of our evolution, distinguishing us from other holding companies [...] We operate in a world where, according to our latest study carried out in 37 countries, 83% of individuals consider entertainment as a vital element in their lives.
>
> (Richebois, 2019)

However, the synergies between Havas and the other subsidiaries are limited to a few experiments of minor importance.

Editis

Editis is a very important player in book publishing in France, the second largest in fact. It has many famous publishing houses, more than 16,000 authors and covers several segments of publishing, including literature, education and pocketbooks: "With six authors in the Top 10 bestsellers in 2019, 50 recognized publishing houses and 4,000 new titles per year, Editis has all the assets to become number 1 in its home market, France. And tomorrow, we will pursue the same international development strategy as for our other subsidiaries", Arnaud de Puyfontaine has stated (Vivendi, 2019: 5). Editis only represents a limited part of Vivendi's turnover, although this is growing.

> Vivendi has fully consolidated Editis since February 1, 2019. Its contribution to Vivendi's sales amounted to €687 million over eleven months, pro forma growth of 6.3% at constant scope and exchange rates compared to the same period of 2018.
>
> (Vivendi, 2019: 206)

"Editis' adjusted operating income (EBITA) has stood at 52 million euros since February 1, 2019, a pro forma growth of 46.9% compared to the same period of 2018, thanks to the increase in turnover and cost control" (Vivendi, 2019: 206).

Editis has three segments.

Literature is the leading segment within Editis, with a turnover of €282 million in 2019. [...] Literature continues to grow (+ 2.0% pro forma eleven months). Editis confirms its leadership position in this segment with six authors in the Top 10 best-selling authors in France in 2019 and also tops many other segments: No. 1 in thrillers, history, youtubers and influencers, and No. 2 in youth, leisure / practical life and tourism (GfK 2019).

(Vivendi, 2019: 206)

The second segment, educational and reference books, achieved a turnover of €184 million in 2019 (ibid.). "Since 1 February 2019, the turnover of the Education & Reference section has risen sharply by 16.8%. Thanks to the reform of Lycée programs, Editis is strengthening its position as a major player in school publishing by relying on its strong brands Nathan, Bordas and Le Robert. The third segment, activities in book marketing and distribution, generated sales of €221 million in 2019" (Vivendi, 2019: 206). This segment plays a very particular role. Books must be distributed from the places where they are printed to the places where they are sold, especially bookstores. Thanks to proactive public policies, France has a very dense network of small bookstores, even outside the larger cities. Unsold books must also be removed from bookstores. This book distribution activity has a very high cost and only major players can become involved in it, providing these services not only for their own publishing houses but also on behalf of external publishers, who do not have such distribution capacities. This is, therefore, quite a profitable activity. "The turnover linked to the distribution of partner publishers is also increasing (+4.2% pro forma eleven months)" (Vivendi, 2019: 206). Thus, Interforum distributes the catalogs of more than 200 French-speaking publishers belonging to Editis as well as those of independent publishers. Present in France, Canada, Belgium, Switzerland and in almost 90 countries around the world, this Editis subsidiary employs more than 1,100 people (Vivendi, 2019: 36). The increase in Editis' turnover is mainly due to external growth operations, that is to say, acquisitions of external companies.

In the second half of 2019, Editis continued its external growth policy with the resumption of the Séguier collection by Robert Laffont, the Agrume collection by Nathan, and the Living School collection by Retz editions, together with, in July 2019, the acquisition of the Archipel group, a publishing house specializing in avant-garde books. In August 2019, Editis also entered the graphic novel and comic book segment, by joining forces with Jungle editions (a subsidiary of the Steinkis group).

(Vivendi, 2019: 206)

The synergies that Editis offers all Vivendi holdings are clearly highlighted in Vivendi's financial communication, particularly regarding the management of intellectual property rights:

> With Editis, Vivendi takes its full place as a cultural entertainment company. Backed by the know-how of the company's other businesses, Editis will have the opportunity to grow and nurture Vivendi's other activities, thus creating a unique ecosystem for IP (Intellectual Properties) talents. Integration is already well underway: many joint projects have already seen the light of day and will continue in 2020.
>
> (Vivendi, 2019: 13)

Arnaud de Puyfontaine, chairman of the Vivendi management board, emphasizes the importance of the property rights held by Editis and the fact that these book rights could be adapted to produce other content, in particular films, series, or video games: "Links have therefore naturally and very quickly multiplied with the rest of our subsidiaries. Two thirds of films and series are inspired by literary works. Editis is our storehouse for stories and franchises!" (Vivendi, 2019: 5). Furthermore, according to Arnaud de Puyfontaine, Editis will naturally find its place within the group because it is involved in talent management. Indeed, talent management is one of the common guiding threads of the various Vivendi subsidiaries:

> 2019 was the year of Editis' integration. A more than successful integration! And this is not surprising: publishing is a creative and talented industry with challenges similar to those of music, audiovisual or video games, where we already have a presence. [...] Its DNA is very close to that of our other entities: entrepreneurial culture, ability to attract the best talent and to constantly reinvent itself to face changes in the sector.
>
> (Vivendi, 2019: 5)

Beyond this financial communication, however, it is clear that collaborations with Vivendi's other subsidiaries remain limited.

Gameloft

Gameloft is a video game development and publishing company. As of 31 December 2019, it had developed 191 video games for smartphones in its 17 studios. The company had an average of 78 million monthly gamers playing its games during 2019. By the end of 2019, more than 2,800 Gameloft developers were working to create downloadable games. Gameloft has developed a large catalog covering different genres: consumer games, action games, sports games, puzzle games, adventure games. Gameloft has a large portfolio of own brands, with franchises such as Asphalt (motor racing), Dungeon Hunter (adventure), Dragon Mania Legends (simulation), Song Pop (musical quiz), Modern Combat, or even Gangstar and World at Arms (action). The franchises cover all genres, then, and are aimed at a wide audience. At the same time, Gameloft is developing a number of games through partnership agreements signed with major rights holders. Specifically, the company works with Disney, Mattel®, Hasbro®, Fox®, Universal, LEGO® and Sega, which allows it to associate some of its games with major international brands: Disney Magic Kingdoms, Minion Rush, Disney Princess Majestic Quest, and LEGO® Legacy: Heroes Unboxed, for example. In 2019, more than 1.5 million Gameloft games were downloaded every day around the world (Vivendi, 2019: 39).

With 1.5 million downloads per day in 2019, Gameloft is one of the world's leading video game publishers. It has different distribution channels. First of all, digital stores accessible from mobiles, tablets and PCs, represent a growing share of sales for mobile applications worldwide. Gameloft is on the Apple (App Store), Google (Google Play), Microsoft (Windows Store) and Amazon (Amazon Appstore) portals and has also distributed its games via several Android platforms in China since 2012. All of these digital stores act as OTT distributors of Gameloft games and the revenues generated are shared between the store and the company. OTT services represented 72% of Gameloft's sales in 2019, and its games are distributed by more than 318 telecommunications operators throughout 110 countries. Subscribers of these operators can buy and download Gameloft games directly on the home screen of their phone when they have been pre-loaded by the phone manufacturer (Gameloft collaborates with Nokia, Samsung, LG, ZTE, Motorola, RIM, Huawei, etc.) or through the operator's digital store. Billing is most often managed by the operator: the cost of the game is included in the consumer's telephone bill or billed via an SMS. Thus, telecommunications operators act as distributors of Gameloft games and the income generated is shared between them and the company. These agreements with operators and phone manufacturers represented 16% of Gameloft's turnover in 2019. In this respect, on behalf of the telephone operators TIM and SFR, Gameloft has developed game distribution applications offering a selection of subscription titles adapted to the age of the players (Vivendi, 2019: 39).

Despite its strengths, the company is struggling, however. In 2019, Gameloft's sales amounted to €259 million, down 11.8% compared with 2018. "In 2019, the fall in Gameloft's fixed costs only partially offset the decline in turnover and increased marketing investments. EBITA stands at €36 million. In 2018, Gameloft's EBITA amounted to just two million euros" (Vivendi, 2019: 207). Gameloft's business models, which primarily offer games for mobile phones, are undergoing renewal. In 2019, sales on OTT platforms, which accounted for 72% of total sales, fell by 11.1%. This decline was largely explained by the delay to 2020 of the three major games initially planned for the second half of 2019 and the saturation of the mobile gaming market. Advertising activity, which represented 11.6% of the total revenue, increased by 4.8% (Vivendi, 2019: 207). Although partnerships with major brands only represent a minority share (a third) of Gameloft's turnover, they are nonetheless significant. At the same time, platforms offer new opportunities.

> Gameloft has generated 65% of its turnover with its own game franchises and 35% with those of large international groups such as Disney and LEGO. Gameloft is now developing its presence on all platforms and has released two games for Nintendo Switch: Modern Combat Blackout and Asphalt 9: Legends.
> (Vivendi, 2019: 207)

The recent subscription-based game distribution model is another growth path for Gameloft. The company developed Ballistic Baseball, one of the first games included on Apple Arcade, Apple's new game subscription service. It has also launched a cloud gaming service, in partnership with Blacknut, which offers operators and manufacturers a catalog of cross-platform games streamed from the cloud (Vivendi, 2019: 207). Mobile games are marketed using a free-to-play business model, which constitutes a major development in Gameloft's economic model, since games are downloadable there for free, which increases download volumes tenfold. These free-to-play games generate income through both the sale of virtual goods, which allow consumers to progress more quickly in the game, and advertising. Gameloft has set up an internal digital advertising network structure, Gameloft Advertising Solutions, which markets advertising space both within its own mobile applications and third-party partner applications. Advertising revenue generated by Gameloft Advertising Solutions represented 12% of the company's revenue in 2019, complementing the revenue from the sale of virtual goods in free games. The amount of mobile advertising investments rose to $190 billion in 2019 from $50 billion in 2015. In 2019, Gameloft had an average daily audience of 9 million players. In addition to traditional advertising formats (banners, interstitials, videos), Gameloft Advertising Solutions also offers innovative formats such as mini games and interactive videos to measure audience engagement rate. Since it owns its inventory, the company creates a safe brand environment, giving the advertiser a perfectly controlled display context. Building on Gameloft's expertise in video game design, Gameloft Advertising Solutions also offers a range of gaming products that allows brands to communicate in a more engaging manner (Vivendi, 2019: 39). Nevertheless, the free-to-free model has its limitations.

> Beyond the free-to-play mobile model, Gameloft is exploring other, more profitable economic models. In 2019, two games were released in parallel on mobile, and Nintendo Switch and Gameloft will soon be present on subscription game distribution platforms. Ballistic Baseball was one of the first games to integrate with Apple Arcade, Apple's new game subscription service. These services will increase in number and become new growth levers for Gameloft.
> (Vivendi, 2019: 13)

Vivendi Village

Vivendi Village is the subsidiary for Vivendi's activities in the performing arts. It is active in festivals, live show productions and theaters. "Through Olympia Production and U Live, Vivendi Village controls ten festivals that have welcomed some 450,000 festivalgoers. The company has bought festivals but also created its own events" (Vivendi 2019: 13).

In 2019, Vivendi Village sales amounted to €141 million euros, up 38.9% at constant scope and exchange rates (14.6% in actual data)

> compared to 2018. Vivendi Village's EBITA represents a loss of €17 million, compared to a loss of €9 million in 2018. If we exclude developing activities in Africa, the adjusted operating profit is practically at breakeven.
>
> (Vivendi, 2019: 208)

The increase in turnover is largely attributable to the development of live performance activities in France and the United Kingdom, as well as venues in France and Africa. Their turnover of €68 million is double that of last year" (Vivendi, 2019: 208).

> This development results in particular from the organic growth of show production activities. It is also explained by acquisitions, in particular that of Garorock (160,000 festival-goers in 2019). Olympia Production has also set up a joint venture with OL Groupe to produce the Felyn Stadium Festival in June 2020 in Lyon.
>
> (Vivendi, 2019: 208)

Among Vivendi Village's assets is an iconic Parisian performance venue, the Olympia, for decades a must-visit musical venue. "Olympia has had a banner year with just over 300 shows. Three new CanalOlympia theaters were opened in Africa in 2019 (14 in total in 10 countries)" (Vivendi, 2019: 208).

In addition to the above, Vivendi introduced dematerialized show tickets in France in 2008. This activity was renamed SeeTickets in 2019 with the acquisition of the British ticketing company See Tickets.

> The ticketing division, federated under the See Tickets brand, represents a turnover of €66 million (+14.4% compared to 2018 and +6.5% at constant scope and exchange rates). This increase can be explained in particular by the development of activities in the United States, where turnover has practically doubled in one year. With the acquisition of Starticket in Switzerland on 30 December 2019, See Tickets is now present in nine European countries and the United States, and sells nearly 30 million tickets per year (25 million in 2019).
>
> (Vivendi, 2019: 208)

In Africa, Vivendi is continuing to develop CanalOlympia cinemas and shows. The network now has 14 theaters and passed the milestone of one million spectators in July 2019. On stage, CanalOlympia has been called upon to host numerous events, while Vivendi Sports organized its first mixed martial arts (MMA) competition in Dakar, Senegal.

(Vivendi, 2019: 208)

In Conclusion, How do Vivendi's Industrial and Financial Strategies Enable It to Offer Dividends to Its Shareholders?

The study of asset disposals and acquisitions and the challenges facing the various subsidiaries leads to the following six observations:

- First, Vivendi's various subsidiaries are all facing profound industrial transformations, essentially linked to the challenges of digital deployment. UMG, the Canal+ Group and Gameloft, but also to a certain extent Vivendi Village, all suffer or benefit from platformization. UMG was able to take advantage of this situation, especially because external stakeholders in the industry, such as Spotify, have developed streaming platforms that have made it possible to monetize UMG's catalog titles. On the other hand, platformization calls into question the industrial positions of the Canal+ Group or Gameloft, with the former being obligated to change its activity to become an aggregator. Likewise, transnationalization takes on very different meanings depending on the subsidiary. Some, like UMG, have truly transnational product lines (the same line in different countries), while others (including Canal+) have a tendency to juxtapose different product lines in different countries. These questions will be explored in more detail in the chapter devoted to cultural issues.
- Second, beyond the discourse of financial communication, it is clear that industrial synergies between the various subsidiaries of Vivendi are very weak. Each of Vivendi's subsidiaries follows dynamics specific to its industry, including transnationalization strategies. Vivendi is therefore a very diversified conglomerate and not a space that promotes industrial synergies.
- Third, the fact that the company does not develop industrial synergies between its various major segments does not mean that Vivendi is not concerned with the industrial sustainability of its subsidiaries when carrying out diversification operations. Various external growth operations have been carried out

within each of Vivendi's subsidiaries. Despite varying greatly in size, they are numerous across all subsidiaries. Some cost only a few million dollars or euros, such as advertising agencies bought by Havas, for example. Others have involved very large amounts, as in the more than 1 billion euros spent on the acquisition of M7 by the Canal+ Group. The ability of each of these external growth operations to create industrial synergies and market power for the benefit of the entire subsidiary should of course be assessed on a case-by-case basis.
- Fourth, the industrial-based and financial dimensions cannot be opposed head-on, since they are subtly intertwined. Admittedly, some assets have been bought and resold quickly at a higher price (as with the participation in the capital of FNAC, for instance). It appears that the most important acquisitions and disposals are primarily aimed at improving the financial situation of the subsidiaries concerned or of the whole company. The example of M7, one of the largest acquisitions carried out by Vivendi in recent years, is relevant in this respect. Purchasing M7 made it immediately possible to extend the scope of the Canal+ Group's activities outside of France and get its hands on a very profitable company, thus automatically improving Canal+ Group's financial results, which have been quite poor in recent years, especially in its historically core business, pay television in France. Nevertheless, the objectives of certain operations are mixed and shifting, such as, for example, Vivendi's rise in the capital of Lagardère, which could represent industrial interests if Vivendi succeeds in securing some of the assets of Hachette, or financial interests if this participation can be sold for profit. Operations that initially appear to have more financial objectives may therefore be of industrial interest later. Likewise, the relationship can be seen from the opposite direction. Industrial operations all have a financial interest and impact. Improving the operating results of the various subsidiaries is an essential condition in maximizing their financial value. Thus, some of them or some of their components can be sold if a disposal opportunity arises. In addition, a positive operating result obviously carries weight in the construction of profit and therefore dividend distribution.
- Fifth, some of these operations may encounter geopolitical issues. The difficult economic relations between French and Italian corporations have led the two governments to support their national industrial players. In this era of globalization and

– within the European Union, economic rivalries still appear to be embedded in relations between nation states.
– Sixth, it is important not to overestimate the constructed nature of these strategies. On the one hand, Vivendi's diversification operations have generally been the result of suddenly occurring opportunities that were not foreseeable. But such plays can produce unpredictable consequences. The example of Bernard Arnault's intervention in the Lagardère operation has already been pointed out. The Elliott fund thwarting Vivendi's takeover bid for Telecom Italia constitutes another example. On the other hand, the outcome of such operations is always uncertain and their cost can be very high, as shown by the acquisitions of holdings in the capital of Mediaset and Telecom Italia. Thus, no strategic industrial vision emerges from this series of operations. The answer to the question asked at the conclusion of the chapter on the history of Vivendi is therefore clear: The company has not chosen to rationalize its strategies around a limited number of industrial core businesses, rather choosing the path of diversification and incessant acquisitions and disposals.

In addition to the above, the overlap between industrial and financial issues appears very clear when we consider the methods by which Vivendi is able to distribute significant dividends to its shareholders. Thus, a diversified capital structure such as Vivendi's is both a socio-economic space in which industrial operations can be conducted over the long term (Vivendi or its "ancestors" have been significant shareholders in Canal+ since its creation) and where these industrial activities can take advantage of the company's financial capacities to grow and a socio-economic space for creating value for shareholders. This financial dimension, present throughout Vivendi's history, has been a primary dimension of the company's strategy since the Bolloré Group took over. It is worth considering just how this value can be passed on to shareholders.

A first observation must be established in this regard. Overall, Vivendi is a profitable company. Admittedly, one of its subsidiaries, UMG, plays a central role in this respect, but Vivendi's overall rate of return, although irregular, is acceptable (as shown in Table 3.4), at least if we compare it with other large French media and entertainment companies. The financial success of Vivendi's various subsidiaries, as well as the presence of one with a very significant EBITA, UMG, allows Vivendi to distribute dividends. Industrial

Table 3.4 Vivendi's main financial indicators (2020–2015)

	2019	*2018*	*2017*	*2016*	*2015*
Revenue (in millions of euros)	15,898	13,932	12,518	10,819	10,762
EBITA (in millions of euros)	1,526	1,288	969	724	942
Total dividend paid to shareholders (in millions of euros)	636	568	499	2,588	2,727
Dividend per share (in euros)	0.50	0.45	0.40	2.00	2.00
Net profit (in millions of euros)	1,583	127	1,218	1,256	697
Profitability rate in relation to turnover (in %)	9.95	0.91	9.73	11.61	6.48

Table created by the author on the basis of data published in Vivendi's activity report.
Source: Vivendi (2019: 184).

power therefore nourishes financial capacity. In return, the fact that Vivendi has a solid financial base makes it possible for it to take industrial risks, particularly in changing activities such as video games (Gameloft) or activities that pose structural difficulties with regard to profitability, such as the performing arts (Vivendi Village). Industrial multi-positioning, failing to generate industrial synergies, generates financial synergies instead, with gains in one activity offsetting the losses recorded in other subsidiaries.

A second observation would be that, unlike with speculative stocks, investors who acquire Vivendi's shares can hardly expect a sharp increase in their value. Indeed, as Table 3.5 shows, Vivendi's share price remained somewhat stagnant between 2015 and 2020. If investors cannot hope for capital gains, then they will expect significant dividend distributions.

The third observation concerns purely financial strategies, which are also essential in order to distribute large dividends. Given the fairly average nature of Vivendi's operating performance, it is therefore very important that the company is able to carry out successful

Table 3.5 Evolution of Vivendi share price from 2015 to 2020

	2020	2019	2918	2017	2016	2015
Vivendi share value at the end of November (November 27 or 28) in euros	25.3	24.9	21.9	22.9	17.6	20

Table created by the author on the basis of financial information published by the financial newspaper *La Tribune*.
Source: *La Tribune*. https://bourse.latribune.fr/webfg/action/VIVENDI/historique.

asset sales operations in order to create value that can be distributed in the form of dividends. In respect of this, the large asset disposals made in the mid-2010s produced significant cash flows. Vivendi then had "about €15 billion in cash after a series of sales in telecoms (SFR, Maroc Telecom, GVT) and video games (Activision Blizzard)" (Challenges, 2015). The American fund, PSAM, which is present in Vivendi's capital, requested the payment of a dividend of €9 billion in the months following the sale of Vivendi's assets in telecommunications. An agreement was concluded between the management of the company and this fund in April 2015 for the distribution of €6.75 billion in dividends to its shareholders by 2017, whereas Vivendi had previously planned to pay out only €4 billion (ibid.). This agreement explains the very high level of dividends during this fiscal year, while the company's profitability fell. Vincent Bolloré had expressed his support for this request from the PSAM fund, and in fact, the Bolloré Group directly and massively benefited from this dividend distribution, it being the main shareholder in Vivendi. While in 2015 the Bolloré Group was experiencing financial difficulties in its core activities, its net income group share increased "by 161% to €564 million euros. An impressive increase, which is largely due to the €325 million net dividends received from Vivendi (€44 million in 2014)" (Dauzat, 2016). The dividend distribution then continued, but at a slower pace because the company no longer had large financial reserves linked to very large asset sales. The amounts of dividends paid remained very significant, however. Vivendi paid €636 million in dividends in April 2019, compared with €568 million in 2018.[2]

Furthermore, Vivendi's share price is supported by a buyback program. This is a common practice, especially among companies not listed among speculative stocks. The reduction in the number of shares makes it easier to increase the dividend per share. A share buyback program was put in place on 28 May 2019. The maximum buyback percentage, initially 5%, was increased to 10% of the share capital by delegation of the management board on 23 July 2019. The aim of the current program is for the company to buy back 130,930,810 shares with a view to repurchasing them for the amount of 115,883,042 shares. The other shares must be distributed in particular to employees (Vivendi, 2019: 180). Finally, it is worth remembering that minority but significant stakes in large companies help maintain Vivendi's share price on the stock market. "As of 31 December 2019, Vivendi held a portfolio of listed minority interests (including Telecom Italia) for a cumulative market value of around €3.95 billion (before taxes)" (Vivendi, 2019: 211).

Like other European players in the media and entertainment industries faced either with market stagnation or a questioning of their industrial positioning due to platformization, Vivendi must develop strategies that enable the company to distribute dividends to its shareholders. Having examined the main industrial and financial strategies employed by the company, in particular from the point of view of industrial synergies and the coexistence of industrial and financial issues, in Chapter 4, we will study these issues further by focusing on political matters, which have been a very important factor in Vivendi's history, from its creation until the present day.

Notes

1 Communication industries gather a heterogeneous set of activities (telecommunications, industries of electronic consumer goods, Web industries and software). Therefore, they include the so-called GAFAMs (Google, Apple, Facebook, Amazon, Microsoft). The companies active in the communication industries have in common to deal with transport, storage and processing of data. In other words, unlike cultural industries, their core business is not in the creation and production of cultural content, even though for the past two decades, they have increasingly entered into the economy of cultural productions for various reasons linked to the affirmation and promotion of their main offer.
2 Source: Vivendi, "Résultats annuels 2019", 13 February 2020, 6. https://www.vivendi.com/wp-content/uploads/2020/07/20200213_VIV_Pres_FY2019_FR.pdf

References

AFP, "Canal+ casse la tirelire pour le distributeur de chaînes M7", *La Tribune*, 28 May 2019. https://www.latribune.fr/technos-medias/medias/canal-casse-la-tirelire-pour-le-distributeur-de-chaines-m7-818607.html

AFP, "Bernard Arnault prend pied au sein du groupe Lagardère", *La Tribune*, 25 September 2020(a). https://www.latribune.fr/entreprises-finance/bernard-arnault-prend-pied-au-sei0c)n-du-groupe-lagardere-858156.html

AFP, "Télécoms: l'Italie va se doter d'un réseau de fibre unique", *La Tribune*, 1 September 2020(b). https://www.latribune.fr/technos-medias/telecoms/telecoms-l-italie-va-se-doter-d-un-reseau-de-fibre-unique-856026.html

AFP, "Vivendi annonce détenir plus de 10% de Lagardère", *La Tribune*, 21 April 2020(c). https://www.latribune.fr/technos-medias/medias/vivendi-annonce-detenir-plus-de-10-de-lagardere-845777.html

AFP and Le Monde, "Canal+ achète le distributeur de chaînes M7 pour un milliard d'euros", *Le Monde*, 27 May 2019. https://www.lemonde.fr/economie/article/2019/05/27/canal-achete-le-distributeur-de-chaines-m7-pour-un-milliard-d-euros_5468278_3234.html

AFP and Reuters, "Le géant chinois Tencent pourrait entrer au capital d'Universal Music (Vivendi)", *La Tribune*, 6 August 2019. https://www.latribune.fr/technos-medias/medias/le-geant-chinois-tencent-pourrait-entrer-au-capital-d-universal-music-vivendi-825291.html

Baudino, Hugo, "Rachat de Havas par Vivendi: Bolloré dans le collimateur de l'AMF", *La Tribune*, 9 September 2017. https://www.latribune.fr/technos-medias/telecoms/rachat-de-havas-par-vivendi-bollore-dans-le-collimateur-de-l-amf-748950.html

Capital Press Room, "Vivendi vend 10% des actions Universal Music (UMG) au géant chinois Tencent", *Capital*, 31 March 2020. https://www.capital.fr/entreprises-marches/vivendi-finalise-la-cession-de-10-dumg-a-un-consortium-mene-par-le-chinois-tencent-1366251

Challenges Press Room, "Vivendi accroît fortement le montant des dividendes versés", *Challenges*, 9 April 2015. https://www.challenges.fr/media/vivendi-accroit-fortement-le-montant-des-dividendes-verses_67800

Dauzat, Olivier, "Bolloré: des résultats 2015 dopés par Vivendi", *Le Revenu*, 3 March 2016. https://www.lerevenu.com/bourse/valeurs-en-vue/bollore-des-resultats-2015-dopes-par-vivendi

Debouté, Alexandre, "Feu vert au rachat d'Editis par Vivendi", *Le Figaro*, 2 January 2019. https://www.lefigaro.fr/medias/2019/01/02/20004-20190102ARTFIG00097-feu-vert-au-rachat-d-editis-par-vivendi.php

De Laubier, Charles, "Ce que prévoit le projet européen MediaForEurope de l'italien Mediaset, contesté par Viveni", *Edition Multimédi@*, 4 February 2020. http://www.editionmultimedia.fr/2020/01/27/ce-que-prevoit-le-projet-europeen-mediaforeurope-de-litalien-mediaset-que-conteste-vivendi/

Dow Jones, "Iliad: Xavier Niel réduit comme attendu sa participation potentielle dans Telecom Italia", *Les Echos Investir*, 19 July 2016. https://investir.lesechos.fr/actions/actualites/iliad-xavier-niel-reduit-comme-attendu-sa-participation-potentielle-dans-telecom-italia-1567564.php

Hélie, Emma, "Vivendi rachète Gameloft: 9 chiffres-clés sur l'éditeur de jeux", *La Tribune*, 21 May 2016. https://www.latribune.fr/technos-medias/informatique/vivendi-rachete-gameloft-9-chiffres-cles-sur-l-editeur-de-jeux-574067.html

La Tribune Press Room, "Vivendi prépare-t-il une OPA sur Telecom Italia?", *La Tribune*, 12 March 2016. https://www.latribune.fr/technos-medias/telecoms/vivendi-prepare-t-il-une-opa-sur-telecom-italia-556480.html

La Tribune Press Room, "Telecom Italia: Rome va exercer ses pouvoirs spéciaux", *La Tribune*, 16 October 2017. https://www.latribune.fr/technos-medias/telecom-italia-rome-va-exercer-ses-pouvoirs-speciaux-754363.html

La Tribune Press Room, "TV: le groupe français Banijay croque le géant Endemol", 26 October 2019. https://www.latribune.fr/technos-medias/contenus-tv-le-groupe-francais-banijay-croque-le-geant-endemol-831699.html

Les Echos Press Room, "Le bénéfice net de Vivendi chute de 35% en 2016", *Les Echos*, 23 February 2017. https://www.lesechos.fr/2017/02/le-benefice-net-de-vivendi-chute-de-35-en-2016-162823

Letessier, Ivan, "Vivendi sort de la Fnac avec une plus-value de 68%", *Le Figaro*, 2 July 2018. https://www.lefigaro.fr/societes/2018/07/02/20005-20180702ARTFIG00330-vivendi-sort-de-la-fnac-avec-une-plus-value-de-68.php

L'Express Press Room and AFP, "Vivendi fait rentrer le chinois Tencent au capital d'Universal Music", *L'express*, 31 December 2019. https://lexpansion.lexpress.fr/actualite-economique/vivendi-fait-rentrer-le-chinois-tencent-au-capital-d-universal-music_2113076.html

Manière, Pierre, "La tornade Vivendi emporte Gameloft", *La Tribune*, 31 May 2016. https://www.latribune.fr/technos-medias/la-tornade-vivendi-emporte-gameloft-575463.html

Manière, Pierre, Maxime Saada (Canal+): "Netflix? Ils sont dans mon camp!", *La Tribune*, 9 November 2018(a). https://www.latribune.fr/technos-medias/telecoms/maxime-saada-canal-netflix-ils-sont-dans-mon-camp-796771.html

Manière, Pierre, "Contrôle de Telecom Italia: affrontement en vue entre Vivendi et Elliott", *La Tribune*, 2 May 2018(b). https://www.latribune.fr/technos-medias/telecoms/controle-de-telecom-italia-affrontement-en-vue-entre-vivendi-et-elliott-777314.html

Manière, Pierre, "Telecom Italia débute la scission de son réseau Internet fixe", *La Tribune*, 28 March 2018(c). https://www.latribune.fr/technos-medias/telecom-italia-debute-la-scission-de-son-reseau-internet-fixe-773462.html

Manière Pierre, "Ubisoft: le clan Guillemot gagne la partie face à Vivendi", *La Tribune*, 21 March 2018(d). https://www.latribune.fr/technos-medias/ubisoft-le-clan-guillemot-gagne-la-partie-face-a-vivendi-772659.html

Manière, Pierre, "Telecom Italia: Vivendi range les armes face à Elliott", *La Tribune*, 29 March 2019. https://www.latribune.fr/technos-medias/telecoms/telecom-italia-vivendi-range-les-armes-face-a-elliott-812549.html

Manière, Pierre, "Vivendi conforté par la justice concernant sa participation dans Mediaset", *La Tribune*, 4 September 2020(a). https://www.latribune.fr/technos-medias/medias/vivendi-conforte-par-la-justice-concernant-sa-participation-dans-mediaset-856386.html

Manière, Pierre, "Vivendi devient le premier actionnaire de Lagardère et change de ton", *La Tribune*, 15 July 2020(b). https://www.latribune.fr/technos-medias/medias/vivendi-devient-le-premier-actionnaire-de-lagardere-et-change-de-ton-852872.html

Manière, Pierre, "Bernard Arnault vient à la rescoussed'Arnaud Lagardère", *La Tribune*, 25 May 2020(c). https://www.latribune.fr/technos-medias/medias/bernard-arnault-vient-a-la-rescousse-d-arnaud-lagardere-848551.html

Manière, Pierre, "L'arrivée de Vivendi jette le trouble sur l'avenir de Lagardère", *La Tribune*, 13 May 2020(d). https://www.latribune.fr/technos-medias/medias/l-arrivee-de-vivendi-jette-le-trouble-sur-l-avenir-de-lagardere-847701.html

Manière, Pierre, "2020, l'année de la reconquête pour Canal+?", *La Tribune*, 3 February 2020(e). https://www.latribune.fr/technos-medias/medias/2020-l-annee-de-la-reconquete-pour-canal-838666.html

Piquard, A., "Pourquoi Orange rafle le contrat des séries HBO", *Le Monde*, 23 March 2017. https://www.lemonde.fr/actualite-medias/article/2017/03/22/pourquoi-orange-rafle-le-contrat-des-series-hbo_5098910_3236.html

Pons, Giovanni, "Alleanza Vivendi-Mediaset, il primo passo a breve", *La Repubblica*, 26 March 2016. https://www.repubblica.it/economia/finanza/2016/03/24/news/alleanza_vivendi-mediaset_il_primo_passo_a_breve-136241865/

Reuters, "Un pacte Vivendi-Amber Capital pour peser sur la gouvernance de Lagardère", *La Tribune*, 11 August 2020. https://www.latribune.fr/entreprises-finance/un-pacte-vivendi-amber-capital-pour-peser-sur-la-gouvernance-de-lagardere-854678.html

Richebois, Véronique, "Havas accélère sur le divertissement en rachetant l'agence américaine Battery", *Les Echos*, 20 June 2019. https://www.lesechos.fr/tech-medias/medias/havas-accelere-sur-le-divertissement-en-rachetant-lagence-americaine-battery-1030972

Ridet, Philippe and Sandrine Cassini, "Vivendi et Mediaset unis pour contrer Netflix", *Le Monde.fr*, 8 April 2016. https://www.lemonde.fr/entreprises/article/2016/04/08/vivendi-fait-son-entree-chez-l-italien-mediaset_4898952_1656994.html

Rosemain, Mathieu and Barzic Gwenaëlle, "Bollore makes first step to merge Vivendi and Havas with 2.4 billion euro deal", *Reuters*, 11 May 2017. https://www.reuters.com/article/us-havas-m-a-vivendi-idUSKBN1872EC

Schmitt, Fabien and Olivier Tosseri, "Telecom Italia: Elliott et Vivendi signent un armistice", *Les Echos*, 29 March 2019. https://www.lesechos.fr/tech-medias/hightech/telecom-italia-elliott-et-vivendi-signent-un-armistice-1005011

Vivendi, "Rapport d'activité annuel", 2019. https://www.vivendi.com/wp-content/uploads/2020/03/20200311-VIV_Vivendi-URD-2019.pdf

Vivendi, "Rapport d'activité annuel", 2018. https://www.vivendi.com/wp-content/uploads/2019/03/20190311_VIV_Vivendi-DDR-2018-Version-finale.pdf

Vulser, Nicole, "Vivendi rachète Editis à l'espagnol Grupo Planeta", *Le Monde*, 16 November 2018. https://www.lemonde.fr/economie/article/2018/11/16/vivendi-rachete-editis-a-l-espagnol-grupo-planeta_5384322_3234.html

4 Vivendi's Political Profile

The dynamics of a large and financialized transnational company active in the media and entertainment industries such as Vivendi raises important and varied political issues. Indeed, the economic, cultural and communication strategies and processes at the heart of Vivendi's business are the result of historical and political construction. The central question in this chapter refers to Vivendi's relations with its social environment. Concretely, this mainly refers to three different political dimensions: the issues of public policies, the governance of Vivendi, and the personality of Vincent Bolloré and his networks of relationships in the political, economic and social spheres.

Vivendi's Activities Raise Numerous Regulatory and Public Policy Issues

Vivendi's activities raise numerous regulatory and public policy issues both at the national level in the various countries where Vivendi's subsidiaries are established and at the transnational level. Of the numerous public policy issues to affect the company, here we will only discuss those in which Vivendi itself has been directly involved. To this end, three public policy issues will be addressed: the French concept of "cultural exception", the strengthening of intellectual property rights and issues related to competition policy.

Issues Related to Intellectual Property Rights Policies

Intellectual property issues play a central role in Vivendi's economy. These issues arise in particular in the relationship between Universal Music Group and streaming platforms, for example. In the field of recorded music, internationally but also in various national contexts, including France, the major record labels have been lobbying governments to adopt repressive anti-piracy legislation like the Digital Millennium Copyright Act (DMCA) in the United States. In France, alongside other players in the music and audiovisual industry, UMG has played a central role in the adoption of the "Creation and Internet Act" (12 June 2009) known as HADOPI (High Authority for the Dissemination of works and Protection of rights on the Internet). This complements a previous Act adopted on 1 August 2006 that covers copyright and related rights in the information society (DADVSI). These Acts transposed a 2001 European directive into French national law and have created many debates in France. The Constitutional Court sanctioned certain legislation contrary to freedom of expression in 2009, including an administrative authority being able to prohibit access to the Internet to a person deemed to be a hacker. UMG continues to actively support this type of regulation for intellectual property rights.

> UMG Recordings and Universal Music Publishing Group (as well as the other major labels and publishers, including Sony and Warner) filed a complaint with United States Communications, Inc. and CoxCom LLC on 31 July 2018 for copyright infringement against Cox Communications, an Internet service and service provider, and its parent company CoxCom, for knowingly inducing and supporting the infringement of copyright by its customers, in contravention of the provisions of the DMCA (Digital Millennium Copyright Act), under which the Internet service provider must put in place a policy of termination of service against its clients who are repeat offenders. At the end of the trial, which took place in December 2019, the jury decided to award all the plaintiffs damages amounting to $1 billion.
>
> (Vivendi, 2019: 310)

Challenges Related to Competition Policy

The competition issues surrounding Vivendi's subsidiaries are linked in particular to dominant positions in defined markets, "relevant markets" as designated by competition law. The disputes between the Italian government and Vivendi have already been discussed in the chapter "Economic Profile". These are linked to both regulating foreign property given issues of national sovereignty and issues of competition law and cross-ownership. Vivendi is notably criticized for owning part or 100% of its significant subsidiaries in two markets considered to be complementary: telecommunications and the audiovisual sector. However, here we will focus on the other competition law issues raised by Vivendi's positions. The Canal+ Group is particularly concerned. Indeed, this company was formed following the acquisitions of major players in the French audiovisual and film market. As a result, it was in a position to control significant market shares and acquire much power in the market. The authorities in charge of regulating competition have thus imposed various constraints on the Canal+ Group in return for acceptance of the acquisition transactions.

The Competition Authority (Autorité de la Concurrence) authorized the acquisition of the advertising financing channels Direct 8 and Direct Star, respectively, renamed "C8" and "CStar", by the Canal+ Group in July 2012. The authorization was renewed in April 2014. Vivendi and the Canal+ Group entered into a series of commitments with the Competition Authority for a period of five years, renewable once. In June 2017, the Competition Authority decided to renew or lift certain commitments, or to adjust others (Vivendi, 2019: 305). The main commitments are as follows: It was decided that the Canal+ Group would enter into framework contracts with two American studios to purchase joint broadcasting rights of films and series for paid and free services (i.e. for advertising financing). On the other hand, in order to limit its market power in France, the Canal+ Group would not have the right to acquire joint broadcasting rights (paid or free services) for more than 20 original French-language films per year. Moreover, C8 and CStar were not allowed to allocate more than 50% of their acquisitions of French film rights to Studiocanal, a subsidiary of the Canal+ Group. This last measure was to prevent the inclusion of C8 and CStar within the Canal+ Group, which would lead to a reduction in purchases from external producers. The Competition Authority reconsiders these authorizations and bans periodically, depending on the challenges that the acquisition continues to pose for the French audiovisual and film market. Another independent authority was also interested in this merger. The Superior Audiovisual Council authorized the repurchase of the chains Direct 8 and Direct Star in September 2012, provided that the Canal+ Group made commitments in terms of program broadcasting, investment obligations and the circulation of rights (Vivendi, 2019: 305).

Another operation also raised competition issues. The two French satellite packages merged when the Canal+ Group took control of Télévision Par Satellite (TPS) at the end of 2005. TPS was a subsidiary of TF1 and M6 at the time. This merger created a monopoly in satellite television, leading at the same time to the Canal+ Group's virtual monopoly of in-pay television in France. The Ministry of the Economy authorized the operation "subject to compliance with commitments made by Vivendi and the Canal+ Group for a maximum period of six years". However, in 2009, the Competition Authority took action and imposed further constraints, considering that the Canal+ Group had not fulfilled its commitments. In 2012, "the Competition Authority again authorized the merger, subject to compliance with 33 injunctions" (Vivendi, 2019: 305). These injunctions and prohibitions related to negotiations for the acquisition of cinematographic rights, the Canal+ Group's sale of its stake in Orange Cinéma Séries (then the only alternative to the Canal+ Group in pay television in France) and to the distribution of a minimum proportion of independent channels. The bans also covered VoD and SVoD. The Authority imposed a ban on acquiring exclusive broadcasting rights of French films for VoD and SVoD and from coupling these rights with others for linear pay-TV, while also restricting the transfer of exclusive VoD and SVoD rights for Studiocanal's French catalog films to the Canal+ Group.

Canal+, Vivendi and the French "Cultural Exception"

The founding of the Canal+ Group raised issues that carried far more weight than the mere existence of the Canal+ channel. Indeed, the founding of Canal+ was paradigmatic of the French cultural exception rule and one of the main means implemented by the French authorities to achieve their objectives within the framework of this policy. Of all the French players in the culture and media industries, Vivendi is the one that has contributed most to the existence of the French cultural exception and, to a certain extent, also the actor to benefit most from this policy. However, Vivendi was also the industrial player that most strongly opposed the constraints imposed by cultural exception, and especially certain public policy measures that limited its ability to freely define its editorial and industrial strategies. Among these constraints opposed by the Canal+ Group are broadcasting quotas and obligations for television channels, and particularly for the Canal+ Group, to financially contribute to the production of French cinema films and television series. This paradox is ongoing in 2020, especially with regard to digital platforms, as will be discussed later.

In order to better understand the position adopted by Vivendi and Canal+ with regard to the cultural exception rule and the regulatory obligations that have weighed on this TV channel, it is necessary to take another look at the history of French audiovisual policy. When public film policy emerged, in particular after the Liberation of France in 1945 and especially after the creation of the Ministry of Culture in 1959 (when the President of the Republic, Charles De Gaulle, appointed André Malraux Minister of Culture), the main objective was to promote quality cinema, so-called "auteur cinema". Furthermore, television was reserved to only a small number of households at that time. General De Gaulle wished to develop and popularize television in order to have a media outlet for his political actions. Indeed, in 1958, he founded a new political regime, the Fifth Republic (still in place in France in 2020). Under this regime, the President of the Republic has a very large amount of power. Television then became the "voice of France", a propaganda tool for General De Gaulle and his government. De Gaulle believed that print newspapers opposed his actions, so he wanted to have a powerful form of media under his control that would allow him to reach the people directly. This was a time when television was heavily controlled and censored. The Ministry of Information did not hesitate to intervene directly in the news. This situation continued with De Gaulle's successor, President Georges Pompidou. It was not until the election of President Valéry Giscard d'Estaing in 1974 that political control loosened somewhat. Giscard d'Estaing was in favor of a more liberal and less interventionist economic policy. He wanted to prepare television for future insertion into the commercial sphere.

Film and television policy changed radically after the Left's arrival in power with François Mitterrand's election as President in May 1981. The objectives of these changes were both economic and political. On the economic front, the new power considered that the economic future no longer lay in activities resulting from the second industrial revolution, but in those linked to culture and creation. In this regard, the conceptions of political power at the time deemed it necessary to promote both the industrial development of these sectors and their commercial dimension. These activities were expected to become one of the main exporting sectors of the French economy, one of the largest employers and the main source of economic wealth. It should be noted that these beliefs largely anticipated British proposals regarding the creative industries and the creative economy in the 1990s. According to the conceptions put forward in particular by the emblematic Minister of Culture at the time, Jack Lang, it was necessary to "reconcile culture and the economy", by which he actually meant reconciling culture and the market economy. In this context, it was necessary to establish powerful industrial players, "French champions". Canal+ was one of the main candidates in this regard, in particular because the audiovisual industry was considered to have the most promising potential, and whose development would therefore be primordial on all levels (turnover, number of jobs and exports).

Canal+ was a political creation, as Bernard Miège (2000) has pointed out. Indeed, the founding of the first and over a long period sole pay-TV channel was conceived, decided and even announced at the highest level of the state. The President of the Republic himself, François Mitterrand, announced the creation of a fourth terrestrial channel in June 1982. Mitterrand then specified that this channel, which was not to be financed by either advertising or by public funds, but by subscription, was to be dedicated to culture. Between 1982 and 1984, when the channel was effectively launched, the project evolved considerably. However, Canal+ has not become a cultural channel, but one dedicated to cinema. The cultural channel was created later and was the predecessor of the current Franco-German cultural channel, ARTE. The French government asked Havas, a major communications company then under its control, to finance the founding of Canal+. This company took on 45% of the capital of Canal+, thus becoming the reference shareholder of the new pay channel. This logic of government intervention was common in France at the time and, to a certain extent, is still practiced in 2020. The government intervenes in the economy indirectly via industrial companies that are legally private, but whose capital is state-owned. This intervention is part of an industrial policy and, in this case, an audiovisual policy. In establishing Canal+, the aim was to build an audiovisual industry encompassing both cinema and the audiovisual sector, even though these two fields were traditionally very distinct in France, as professions and businesses, and in terms of public policies. The objective of this cultural policy was therefore mainly economic, attributing economic objectives to cultural policies being new in France in the 1980s. What was also new was the Ministry of Culture being interested in cultural industries precisely due to their industrial dimension. Canal+ was therefore the first private terrestrial television channel to be created in the country, there having previously been only three public terrestrial channels in France. One of them, TF1, was privatized in 1987. In addition, two other private commercial terrestrial channels were created in 1985 and 1986, as television underwent a process of commodification. The objective was to promote freer forms of audiovisual culture than the very conservative and censored content previously offered by public television. Commercial television was considered as less prone to censorship and conservatism than its public counterpart. Thus, Canal+'s mission was to invent a new editorial line that was neither conservative nor elitist, was open to a large audience and would help produce a "modern" type of content that could be exported. HBO was one of the models it would follow.

At the same time, film policy was being profoundly revised in France. Between 1982 and 1984, negotiations were undertaken with the representative institutions of the cinema industry so that Canal+ could contribute to the dynamism of French film production, and at the same time have access to exclusive quality content. The objective here was to strengthen independent cinematographic production. Independent producers are actually independent from TV channels, and to be considered as such there must be no capital links between a producer and the television channels. According to this new policy, Canal+ was obligated (and it still was in 2020) to acquire broadcasting rights for films without being considered the co-producer. In other words, the television channels had to finance a large part of the production cost of films (and also of "audiovisual works", including television series and documentaries), but did not acquire any property rights over this content. The producers remained the sole owners. Thanks to these cross-subsidies, this policy was only marginally financed by state subsidies. Canal+ has in fact constituted the main tool in this public policy. The company has been the main financial contributor to French film production. In return, Canal+ obtained the rights to broadcast these films before other channels, and these exclusive rights over the latest films have greatly contributed to the channel's appeal to potential subscribers.

The principle of production financing obligations applied to Canal+ has also been applied to new private channels as well as public service channels. Following the creation of Canal+, and while the television industry was undergoing strong growth in France, albeit with an increasingly commercial bent, the public authorities wanted to control the audiovisual sector by developing a whole set of regulations. The obligations to finance audiovisual production weighing on TV channels were explicitly provided for in the Act passed on 30 September 1986 relating to "freedom of communication", which aimed to expand the liberalization of the audiovisual sector. These obligations were reinforced by government decree in 1990 and extended to new emergent forms of non-linear television in 2007. Other measures have also been taken. The regulation of relations between "distributors" and film and audiovisual producers involves a very complex set of interrelated rules in France. These form a "system", and it is difficult to challenge any of these rules without threatening this entire regulatory system. It should also be noted that the distinction between cinema on the one hand and what is deemed to be the audiovisual sector (television) on the other hand still exists in France, in terms of the industry, professional careers and regulations. Although television regulation has been built on the film regulation model, the rules being based on the same founding principles, there are some important rules that apply only to cinema. The same organization governs all regulations: the National Center for Cinema and Animated Image (CNC). Without going into further detail, the main rules and those that most concern Canal+ are as follows: First, television channels must devote part of their turnover to ordering programs from producers, and a significant part of these orders must be placed with the so-called independent producers. TV channels only acquire broadcasting rights and do not own the content they pay for. Cinema films or audiovisual content therefore remain the property of producers. These regulations are in place for both cinema and the audiovisual sector. This is the heaviest obligation on Canal+, involving high amounts. Indeed, in this respect, Canal+ must make greater financial contributions than other large channels, those with advertising funding. France Télévision (excluding France 5), TF1 and M6 must devote 3.2% of net sales from the previous financial year to the production of European cinematographic works, including 2.5% to original French cinematographic works. In contrast, Canal+ must devote 12% and 9%, respectively, to the acquisition of broadcasting rights for European cinematographic and original French works. At least 80% of the obligation to produce original French works must relate to pre-purchases (exclusive rights acquired before shooting begins), and three quarters of the expenditure on the latter should benefit independent production. Second, regulation imposes broadcasting quotas for European cinematographic and original French works. Out of the total annual number of broadcasts and reruns of cinematographic works, all television services must reserve at least 60% for European works and 40% for original French ones. Third, the successive release of the media through which the films are marketed is regulated, this being known as "film windowing" or "media chronology".[1] The first valuation window is when the film is shown in movie theaters, followed by various media according to an order fixed within the framework of an inter-professional agreement, i.e. established following negotiations between the various stakeholders (distributors and producers) under the watchful eye of the CNC. In the last version to be adopted, the succession of the various media is established over 46 months. These rules aim to preserve the attractiveness of cinemas by reserving new films for them. A 10.72% tax is levied on all cinema tickets sold in France. The funds collected through this tax go to the CNC and help finance its policies. These so-called media chronology rules in France also reserve a privileged place for Canal+. Films whose production Canal+ has contributed financing to can be broadcast fairly quickly by this channel, after just three or eight months, depending on their success in theaters. Thus, Canal+ benefits from an advantage compared with other channels, which must wait longer before broadcasting films. Furthermore, SVoD platforms cannot broadcast films until 36 months after their theatrical release.

This public policy somehow endured for 30 years, despite opposition from Canal+ since the end of the 1990s. Vivendi's attempts to question this French "cultural exception" rule and, in particular, to attack the obligations upon television channels in favor of cinema and audiovisual production have undergone three main phases, during each of which there has been a deepening of transnationalization in the audiovisual industry. The inclusion of Canal+ within French national regulations has always been perceived and presented by managers of the Canal+ group and Vivendi as a hindrance to the company in the face of these competitors, meaning an obstacle to competition and an advantage for the company's foreign competitors.

The first phase of attacks came when Canal+ was integrated within Vivendi and Vivendi became Vivendi Universal thanks to the acquisition of very important audiovisual assets in the United States. Canal+ no longer had a great need for French content, especially cinematographic content. Vivendi Universal had its transnational strategies and Canal+ was a part of them. The goal was to import content that Vivendi's American subsidiaries were producing into France and Europe. Thus, although the public authorities had created it to become the French industrial champion, Canal+ had become integrated within Vivendi Universal and escaped the bosom of the state. The cultural exception rule was therefore a problem for such a transnationalized player. Part of Vivendi Universal's strategy, then, was to make Canal+'s main role that of the distributor of American content in France and Europe, and no longer a producer of French content. As mentioned above, the financing obligations of French cinematographic productions have always represented a very heavy financial burden for Canal+, which appeared far more as a constraint than as an advantage.

Jean-Marie Messier's statement against cultural exception in general and these obligations in particular was made during the announcement of Vivendi Universal's takeover of USA Networks and was taken as a provocation in France by both audiovisual and cinematographic producers and among those responsible for public cultural policies. Indeed, this takeover of a major player in the American cinema and television industry represented a major change in the transnational strategies adopted by the company. This acquisition allowed the emergence of a new transnational giant in the audiovisual industry, Vivendi Universal Entertainment (VUE), making Vivendi Universal the world's second-largest player in the cultural and media industries. In France, the creation of VUE was perceived as a threat to the French audiovisual industry, especially by producers, who feared that the management board at Vivendi Universal would put pressure on the public authorities to reduce or even eliminate its regulatory obligations. And this fear was justified, as Jean-Marie Messier developed a lobbying campaign to attack French policies on cinema and the audiovisual sector, and especially the obligations on Canal+. He called for an end to the cultural exception rule the French had insisted on including in the Marrakech agreements that founded the World Trade Organization in 1994, claiming that cultural exception opposed cultural diversity.

> Responding [according to Messier] to the fear of certain producers and filmmakers from France who questioned an 'Americanization of French cinema', Vivendi's leader bluntly rejected all criticism: 'The French cultural exception is dead, and French anguish is archaic', he said.
>
> (Rousselot, 2001)

Messier emphasized the power of a globalized industrial group in achieving cultural objectives, and particularly cultural diversity, while he considered cultural exception a vestige of the past, from times preceding globalization. Presenting Vivendi Universal as the champion of cultural diversity, he stressed that the free market not only respected diversity but actually went further than that. He stressed that Vivendi was able to offer differentiated cultural products and thereby promote cultural diversity due to its industrial and financial power. According to this view, policies are less efficient than the free market. Without making explicit reference to them, Messier was invoking earlier works from economic theory. Based on game theory, Harold Hotelling (1929) had attempted to demonstrate that economic actors competing with each other through the differentiation of their products may all have an interest in offering products that correspond to average tastes, or in other words, in only offering a low diversity of products rather than very differentiated ones. Peter O. Steiner (1952) applied this perspective to show that a monopoly situation in the radio industry favors diversity, while competition encourages the various stations to all offer the same type of programming corresponding to the supposed tastes of the most important segment of radio listeners.

There is a profound attachment to cultural exception in France, shared far beyond the real main beneficiaries of its policies, that is, film and audiovisual producers. Most politicians, whether left or right-leaning, are unconditionally in favor of the cultural exception rule. All cultural actors and most citizens also support it, as it constitutes one of the foundations of the contemporary conception of the French nation (Bouquillion, 2019). A French lawyer, Serge Regourd, established a link between the principle of cultural exception and that of public service (as it is understood in France). As he noted:

> The notion of cultural exception seems to have its roots in an old background of social representations relating to the "French exception" itself, representations already built on a specific conception of the relations between the state and the market – on a certain conception of The Republic, at the heart of the "republican pact" forged under the Third Republic and already postulating what General de Gaulle would later describe as a "certain idea of France" integrating a voluntary public action and refusal of submission to the American imperial power. In this context, the national interest is only one of the declensions of the general interest, itself constituting the framework of what will later be called "social ties". [...] France has constructed the doctrine of public service as a model of socio-political organization, one of the components of French identity.
> (Regourd 2004: 19)

The questioning of the exception by a former senior official running a company that had been built by the public authorities in order to serve as the French national champion, especially against the American giant players in the media and entertainment, therefore appeared to be the height of betrayal. The construction of cultural exception as a founding national myth is so strong in France that public debate, and even political reflection itself, has become extremely difficult. This myth actually hides the lobbying power of film producers in France, who have succeeded in obtaining protective regulation for their activity from the public authorities by mobilizing star actors and winning over the support of public opinion. Lobbying began very early in the history of French cinema. In the 1920s, quota restrictions were adopted on the entry of American films into France. The Blum-Byrnes agreements, which were concluded in 1946 and opened French borders to American films in return for obtaining Marshall aid, were revised under pressure from French producers and movie stars in 1948 to limit the entry of American films into the French market. As mentioned earlier, in 1994, French negotiators imposed the cultural exception rule in return for France's signing of the Marrakesh Agreements, founding the World Trade Organization (WTO).

From the 1960s onwards, the objectives of cinema lobbyists were less aimed toward closing borders and more toward obtaining greater funding for movie production. The widespread acceptance of cultural exception made it politically difficult to draw up an assessment of these policies in favor of cinema and the audiovisual industry. Likewise, in France, little thought is given in political and regulatory circles to the new challenges that transformations in the cultural industries linked to globalization, financialization and the deployment of digital technology pose to public policies, and particularly since the rise in transnational products from both Advertising Video on Demand (AVoD) and Subscription Video on Demand (SVoD) platforms during the 2010s. Debates on Canal+ and Vivendi's transnational strategies have revealed how difficult it is to approach these issues rationally in France.

Vivendi requested an end to its regulatory obligations a second time when new audiovisual services suppliers emerged on the market. Indeed, these players in the non-linear television sector were not subject to the same rules as the historical audiovisual players, which generated a distortion in terms of competition, as historical players like Canal+ pointed out. However, the public authorities tried to maintain the existing obligations and, as far as possible, extend them to new entrants. The stakes were high for audiovisual and cinema companies in France, both those who financed (broadcasters) and those who received the funds (producers). In the early 2010s, financing obligations represented very significant sums of money. For instance, the total amount collected in the form of contributions from the audiovisual sector (excluding cinema) totaled €837.6 million in 2013. This amount was also significant in relation to the turnover of audiovisual service providers, whose taxable base totaled €6.34 billion that same year (Conseil Supérieur de l'Audiovisuel, 2013). Professional agreements between "service publishers" (broadcasters) and other organizations representing audiovisual production were signed in October 2008 and in February 2010. The regulatory obligations of expenditure in production which weigh on the television channels and platforms are, in part, the result of negotiations between the television channels and platforms on the one hand and union representatives of cinema and television producers on the other hand. They agree to set the levels (in relation to the turnover of each channel) and conditions for these expenses. Then, once the agreements between the two parties are signed, the regulatory authorities endorse these agreements and are responsible for enforcing them. For other parties, these regulatory obligations regarding expenditure on production are established by the regulatory authorities in specifications authorizing the creation of television channels. The public authorities succeeded in obtaining such agreements from historical actors and new entrants alike, including the historical French telecommunications operator, Orange. The existing relationship was then extended to non-linear television, with historical players having to agree to continue fulfilling their various obligations.

However, from the beginning of the 2010s onwards, the economic situation of the historical audiovisual players deteriorated markedly in France for various reasons (a fall in television advertising budgets, increased competition between various types of audiovisual services, competition of audiovisual services by different types of digital services, etc.). Consequently, the turnover of these companies started to stagnate. Conversely, the revenues of transnational actors in the digital industries or electronic equipment manufacturers were growing, while some of them were developing legal or illegal audiovisual products without being subject to French regulatory constraints. The historic French audiovisual players therefore once again challenged the legitimacy of the regulation, which weighed on them but not their new foreign competitors. Canal + questioned this regulation for the third time. The height of this dispute is linked to Netflix's entry onto the French market in 2014. Competition from Netflix was of course more direct and on a much larger scale than that of foreign competitors, the former establishing head-on competition with Canal+. Unlike YouTube, for example, Netflix, which had a position in SVoD, competed with Canal+ in its core business, that of pay television. After Netflix's entry into the French market, it became clear that the audiovisual industries were going to enter a phase of profound change and that other operators would also take the same path as Netflix sooner or later. These other players were not subject to the same obligations because their European headquarters were not in France (Netflix's headquarters was in the Netherlands). Thanks to European law, they could legally operate in France without contributing to the financing of production and without respecting the quota of 60% original European and 40% French works. Thus, the Canal+ management board emphasized the need to remove or lighten these obligations in order to allow it to survive in the context of the new transnationalized platform economy. This evolution in terms of regulation would therefore be the *sine qua non* condition for preserving the French film and television industries and their main player, Canal+.

On 25 May 2016, the European Commission adopted a draft revision of the Audiovisual Media Services Directive (AVMS), which envisages compelling video-on-demand platforms to comply with the regulations not of the countries from which they broadcast but those of the receiving countries. This prospect materialized with the effective revision of the directive. The revision of the services directive of audiovisual media adopted on 14 November 2018, "Audiovisual media services", imposes two series of new obligations on providers of audiovisual media services, related to expenditure on production, on the one hand, and distribution of European and national audiovisual and cinematographic works, on the other hand. One of these major changes is that the country of origin principle, stemming from Directive 2010/13 / EU of 10 March 2010, is being supplanted by the law of the country of destination. Thus, with the transposition of the "Audiovisual Media Services" (AVMS) directive into French law, it was decided that foreign SVoD players must comply with various obligations, they now being required to spend 25% of their turnover on expenses in production. These obligations only apply to services with a turnover of at least €5 million. There is also a plan to stipulate that their catalog must contain at least 30% European works (Dalloz, 2020). In return for their expenditure on French production, the rules of "film windowing" are being changed for production funding obligations that will be imposed on foreign platforms such as Netflix or Disney+. At the time of writing, in December 2020, this matter is under negotiation. Extension of the regulatory constraints to foreign players has thus allowed the authorities to counter the opposition strategies adopted by the historical French audiovisual players, Canal+ in particular. One question that still remains very contentious is that regarding the share of independent production in the expenditure on production obligations[2]. Maxime Saada, president of the Canal+ Group, declared: "Today, we could produce a lot more if we had more rights to the series that we finance, then we would be in the same competitive situation as Netflix' […]" (Piquard, 2019).

By combining channels' voluntary expenditures (in particular on the production of content they will own) and that imposed by regulation, the amounts of contributions made by television channels to audiovisual and film production were very high at the end of the 2010s in France. By 2017, the share of television channels in financing film production based on a percentage of their turnover remained very high, representing 36.6% of the production costs for original French films, and 70% of the cost of the series they produce. In the same year, the overall amount of expenditure retained for contributions to audiovisual production (excluding films) amounted to €863.4 million. The four historical audiovisual groups (France Télévisions, TF1, M6 and Canal+) accounted for 91% of this. France Télévisions was the main contributor (48% of declared expenditure, or €409.9 million). The amounts linked to films were lower than those spent on "audiovisual" productions. In the aforementioned year, contributions to the production of cinematographic works amounted to €371.3 million, of which 80% was pre-financing of European cinematographic and original French works (Ministry of Culture and Communication, 2020). Canal+ was not the main financier of audiovisual production, but rather the one to contribute least, the company having paid only €87 million compared with €410 million from the public service (France Télévisions), €172 million from TF1, and €114 million from M6. However, Canal+ was the leading audiovisual player in financing film production in 2017, making a contribution of €195 million, while France Télévisions contributed only €61 million, TF1 €42 million, OCS (Orange) €38 million and M6 €24 million. However, among these total expenses, the amounts, which are strictly linked to regulatory obligations, tend to decrease due to the drop in turnover of the incumbent audiovisual players. This has particularly affected Canal+, which under the compulsory regulations spent €211 million in 2013, while in 2019 it financed 109 original French-language films for an amount of €100.7 million (Vivendi, 2019: 58).

> On 8 November 2018, the Canal+ Group announced the renewal of its agreement of 7 May 2015 with all professional cinema organizations (ARP, BLIC and BLOC), thus extending the historic partnership of over thirty years between Canal+ and French cinema until 31 December 2022. Under the terms of this agreement, Canal+ is required to invest 12.5% of its income in the financing of European cinematographic works each year. In audiovisual matters, Canal+ must devote 3.6% of its total annual net resources to expenditure each year.
> (Vivendi, 2019: 269)

Thus, despite the opposition of historical players including Canal+, the public authorities have succeeded in preserving the regulations that include expenditure obligations in production. However, these compulsory expenses, and particularly those pertaining to Canal+, are in an inexorable decline today due to competition from SVoD platforms.

Vivendi's Governance

Vivendi used to be a limited company (SA) listed on Euronext, Paris. Governance raises political issues linked on the one hand to the type of control of the company[3] and on the other hand to the networks of relations it has with other companies or institutions, formed through the composition of the company's management boards.

The French political and economic circles were alarmed by the founding of Vivendi Universal some 20 years ago, fearing the company would fall under the control of American interests. Indeed, the numerous acquisitions of assets overseen by Jean-Marie Messier in the United States were partly financed by the granting of shares in the company. Thus, the share of American industrial interests in Vivendi's capital did gradually rise. At the same time that Vivendi was becoming a speculative stock, American investment funds also entered its capital. This violated a rule of public policy. In France, it is forbidden for a non-French actor or, since the constitution of the European Union, for a non-European actor, to hold more than

20% of the capital of a company that operates wireless networks. Foreign interests clearly owned more than 20% of Vivendi, particularly American ones, while Vivendi controlled Canal+, this channel operating a terrestrial television network. At that time I met with an official from the Conseil Supérieur de l'Audiovisuel (Bouquillion, 2004). He acknowledged that the rule was not being respected, but considered it not to be a problem, seeing this rule of limiting foreign ownership as a legacy of the past. The rule was imposed for reasons of national security, to prevent a hostile foreign power from controlling the terrestrial spectrum and therefore the radio stations (prior to television). Even if it was not important in strictly regulatory terms, many economic decision-makers and politicians worried that this symbol of French capitalism in the media and entertainment world would come under American control. These historical circumstances partly explain why Vincent Bolloré was so easily able to take control of Vivendi, without much opposition. French political circles welcomed the fact that Bolloré was French and was keeping Vivendi under French control. And, indeed, Bolloré still exerts close control over Vivendi to this day.

The rise of the Bolloré Group in Vivendi's capital occurred gradually. At the beginning of 2004, the group took a 36.2% stake in Havas. Ten years later, in October 2014, it launched a takeover bid that led to it having a 72.81% control of that company (La Tribune, 2015). The former head of Havas, Alain de Pouzilhac, resigned in June 2005 and Vincent Bolloré became chairman. In 2015, Yannick Bolloré, Vincent's son, took over as chairman. Havas had merged with Vivendi back in 2000. Some of its assets, including advertising, were subsequently transferred from Vivendi to a separate new company. In April 2012, as rumors suggested a raid was being prepared against Vivendi, Vincent Bolloré took advantage of the low share price to acquire a stake in Vivendi's capital. The Bolloré Group sold two commercial TV channels to Vivendi, Direct 8 and Direct Star, in exchange for a 1.7% stake. At the same time, the Bolloré Group also acquired 2.2% of Vivendi, raising its stake to 5%. In March 2015, it acquired new shares and then held 8.15% of the voting rights. The Bolloré Group subsequently continued to increase its stake in Vivendi's capital. Since 2017, Vivendi has become a subsidiary of the Bolloré Group. Indeed, the group has fully consolidated Vivendi since April 26, 2017, while Vivendi has become an important source of income for the group. On 18 April 2019, the group received a dividend of €165 million (compared with 1 of €134 million for the financial year 2017, paid in 2018) (Vivendi, 2019: 299). Holding onto

Vivendi has become very important for the Bolloré Group, which is experiencing difficulties in some of its activities, in particular electric cars, batteries and transport. Although the group had a turnover of €24.843 million in 2019, its EBITA was largely achieved thanks to Vivendi. While several activities had a negative EBITA, that of the "Communication" segment, i.e. Vivendi, amounted to €1,526 million, the largest in the group. The segment "Transport and logistics" recorded an EBITA of €580, while the Bolloré Group as a whole had an EBITA of €1,634 million in 2019 (Bolloré, 2019: 6). Finally, the group's market capitalization was just €9.83 billion as of 9 November 2020 (source: Yahoo Finance).

No single shareholder owns enough Vivendi shares to have a majority control of the company. However, despite its minority stake, the Bolloré Group does have strong control over the company, giving it enough power to guide its management and maximize the distribution of dividends to shareholders, the primary beneficiary of dividend distributions being the group itself. Vivendi's shareholder base is relatively stable, although the Bolloré Group's stake has seen a gradual rise. It held 26.07% of the capital as of 31 December 2019 and 29.64% of the voting rights, compared with 20.51% and 29.56% as of 31 December 2017, respectively. The second-largest shareholder is a large historical French bank, Société Générale. It held 5.29% of the capital and 4.98% of the voting rights as of 31 December 2019 (up from 4.79% and 4.10% on 31 December 2017, respectively). The third-largest shareholder is a group formed by the Caisse des Dépôts et Consignations and the Public Investment Bank, two public institutions that serve as privileged tools of the French state for intervention in the economy. This group held 3.23% of the capital and 3.11% of the voting rights on 31 December 2019 (up from 2.99% and 2.62% on 31 December 2017, respectively). Vivendi employees held 2.95% of the capital and 4.07% of the voting rights as of 31 December 2019 (up from 2.75% and 3.75% as of 31 December 2017, respectively). The other shareholders all held less than 1% of the company's capital as of 31 December 2019. As can be observed from these figures, Vivendi's shareholder structure is dominated by French interests, at least with regard to identified shareholders. The so-called free-float shareholding represented 59.99% of the capital and 56.57% of the voting rights on 31 December 2019 (source: Vivendi, 2019: 184). Therefore, although the Bolloré Group exercises a minority control over Vivendi, no other shareholder has a significant number of shares to oppose the leaders of the group and wrestle control from them, even if a takeover bid is always possible.

In 2020, Vivendi's governance structures are firmly in the grip of Vincent Bolloré and his family, and are divided not a supervisory board, which defines the main directions of the company's strategy, and a management board, which has executive powers. The former therefore examines and decides on the strategic orientations of the company, exercising permanent control over the management implemented by the latter and authorizing major operations with regard to acquisition, disposal or internal restructuring, or any likely to have an impact on the group's financial structure, as well as strategic partnership agreements (Vivendi, 2019: 105). Vivendi's 2019 activity report (105–106) highlighted Yanick Bolloré's qualities, international influence and media industry experience, underlining the personal qualities that the leader of a large group must have, while also stressing his being a member of the Bolloré family. In addition to the principle of the leader that will be presented below, it also mentions another principle – that of the reference family shareholder, which represents a guarantee of security.

> Mr. Yannick Bolloré benefits from a transversal approach to Vivendi's businesses, on content, media and communication, and from the experience of integrating a world-class industrial group. His was thus considered the best profile to guide Vivendi in pursuing its strategy. This decision demonstrates the supervisory board's confidence in the structuring vision of its benchmark family shareholders, a guarantee of stability and the future for the group and for its talents, but also for all shareholders and other stakeholders.

Vivendi's supervisory board had 12 members as of 31 December 2019, including three members of the Bolloré family: Vincent, as "*censor*" (an honorary title), Yannick as chairman and Cyrille (another of Vincent's sons). The board does not currently have any prominent figures from French or international capitalism. The only foreigner, although not employed by Vivendi, is Katie Stanton, who is of American nationality. She is the founder and general partner of Moxxie Ventures, an early stage venture capital firm based in San Francisco and was formerly the vice president of Global Media at Twitter. A member of the Dassault family, Laurent Dassault, joined the supervisory board in March 2020. The Dassault group is a large French aeronautics company, mainly manufacturing military aircraft. Laurent is the only link to major industrial players outside Vivendi. In other words, there are no prominent figures to question the power of the Bolloré family on the supervisory board.

Also, Vivendi does not appear to have links with alliance networks, either nationally or internationally. According to commentators, Vincent Bolloré is preparing his departure, scheduled for the bicentenary of the Bolloré Group during 2022. His son Yannick will become fully responsible for Vivendi and his other son, Cyrille, for the Bolloré Group (Beaufils, 2019). As of 31 December 2019, Vivendi's management board was still headed by Arnaud de Puyfontaine. It has seven members, all important executives at the company, including Vincent Bolloré's nephew, Cédric de Bailliencourt, who is also the vice-president of the Bolloré Group's board.

Vincent Bolloré, His Personal and Family History and Links with the French Political Sphere

Vincent Bolloré is a well-known French businessman, who had the 17th largest fortune in France in 2020, with assets valued at €5.7 billion on 3 September 2020 (Challenges, 2020). He is a very important figure in French capitalism, with significant links to major French political figures. Just as we have studied the career of Jean-Marie Messier, it is also essential to dissect that of Vincent Bolloré. In this age of financialization, financial communication is essential. The management of the company must give credit to the idea that "there is someone at the helm", a "boss". This leader must possess qualities that are unlikely to be united in one person, however, namely, both visionary and budgetary discipline. From a financial communication perspective, the ideal leader should possess the qualities of both a guru and an accountant (Bouquillion, 2008), it being essential that the financial and specialized press adopt these representations. The ability to raise funds and enter into partnerships depends to a significant extent on the leader's image and the belief that person can instill in others. In the past, for instance, the transformation of Vivendi into Vivendi Universal was facilitated by Jean-Marie Messier's ability to convince the Bronfman family that his project was viable. In more sociological terms, a leader's social capital is essential to enjoy success at the helm of the company. This social capital can then be converted into economic capital in the sense that it makes it easier for the company to conclude transactions. It generates trust, which is essential in financial matters.

Vincent Bolloré does not lack social capital. Born in 1952, he comes from the industrial and financial upper bourgeoisie. His maternal grandmother, Nicole Goldschmidt, was a resistance fighter during the Second World War, having joined General De Gaulle in

London. She herself hailed from a very old banking family allied to the Rothschilds and Bischoffsheims. Through her, Vincent Bolloré is therefore linked to the upper spheres of European capitalism. His father's family, on the other hand, is Breton industrialists, who founded the Bolloré Group back in 1822. Unlike other former executives of Vivendi, Vincent Bolloré did not graduate from a "Grande Ecole". He was educated at university, obtaining both Master's and doctorate degrees. Bolloré considerably developed the family business after joining it in the early 1980s. Previously, in the 1970s, he was the deputy director of Compagnie Financière, a major and influential French investment bank owned by Edmond de Rothschild.

During his career, he has reached a national and even, in some ways, international position, having managed several corporate buyouts that have ensured success for the Bolloré Group. In the early 2000s, Bolloré was part of the takeover of Mediobanca, a major Italian investment bank, alongside other players including Unicredit, which became Mediobanca's largest shareholder. In 2018, he retired from the shareholders' agreement.

> Bolloré's presence has long been seen as a Trojan horse to penetrate Italy, where the group is also present through its holdings in Telecom Italia and Mediaset. With 7.9% of the capital, he remains Mediobanca's second largest shareholder after Uni-Credit (8.4%).
>
> (Tosseri, 2018)

The Bolloré Group also has a particularly strong presence in Francophone Africa. In addition to rubber plantations and palm oil activities, it is a leader in logistics. The company controls ports such as Abidjan (Ivory Coast), Conakry (Guinea) and Misrata (Libya) (AFP, 2014). Many of its activities are related to the political sphere, especially through public procurement.

Vincent Bolloré is a friend of the former French president, Nicolas Sarkozy. After Sarkozy had just been elected president, Vincent Bolloré lent him his private jet and yacht so that the new president could take a rest, thus sparking a scandal. Bolloré denied the facts at first, before ultimately acknowledging them to be true. However, he also declared:

> It is moreover a tradition in the Bolloré family, who had the opportunity to receive Léon Blum for several weeks in his mansion, on his return from captivity [after the Second World War],

or Mohammed V [former King of Morocco at the time of the independence of this country] on return [from exile] from Madagascar before he became king of Morocco.

(Le Monde, 2007)

In saying this, Bolloré wanted to highlight the social capital of his family as a source of prestige. It was a way of presenting a practice that some considered to be out of place as an ancient tradition. In 2013, he also declared his friendship for Bertrand Delanoë, the socialist mayor of Paris, who had chosen to provide Parisians with electric cars built by Bolloré for micro-rentals (Autolib program). He announced his support for Delanoë's successor as mayor, Anne Hidalgo, also a socialist, before entering into a conflict with her after the failure of Autolib in 2018.

From the early 2000s onwards, the Bolloré Group sought to invest in the media sector, with Vincent Bolloré attempting several unsuccessful hostile takeovers of TF1, the main French commercial television channel. At that time, TF1 was seen as a very important opinion leader. An assertion common among journalists, it was particularly based on the fact that in the 1990s the TF1 news was the most watched by the French, enjoying around 40% of the audience share. Various journalistic investigations have supported this point of view and have also studied the occult relationship between high-level French politicians and the leaders of Groupe Bouygues (construction and civil engineering), the main shareholder of TF1. The best known is the one conducted by Pierre Péan and Christophe Nick (1997). Although TF1 was a profitable channel at the time, it was also a formidable means of political influence. According to a very widespread belief in the 1990s, TF1 had a heavy influence on the elections for the Presidency of the Republic.

This chapter has underlined the importance of Vivendi's political dimension. Whether supporting or opposing public policies, they bring a weight to bear on the structuring of various cultural industries, in particular music or the audiovisual sector in France, a country where the largest national player in media and entertainment contributes to the construction of national culture. In addition, the political dimension is also at the heart of operations carried out by a major financialized industrial player such as Vivendi. Although public policies can both pose constraints and offer opportunities, the governance of this company is also a political act insofar as it concentrates power relations. Hence, its head also has an eminently political role. This person's personal or family networks must make it possible to ensure the benevolence of political power. Likewise, his or her personality is also essential in building the company's appeal to financial players. In short, the political dimension is not external to economic realities. On the contrary, it constitutes one of the most important aspects of the company. All that remains for us to study now is Vivendi's specifically cultural dimension.

Notes

1 The central idea of "film windowing" is that the successive release of a film in the media is regulated. The rules are different for each country. In France they are very specific, it being the country with the longest period for a film's full release (44 months from the first theatrical release, according to rules established in 2018). This regulation has two objectives. The first is to distinguish between several valuation windows, theoretically to maximize the total valuation of the film. The second objective is to "reward" distributors such as Canal+ who most fund the production of films in accordance with their regulatory obligations. Indeed, French regulations force television channels to spend large sums on the production of films or series in proportion with their turnover. However, this varies by channel. Canal+ must spend more on film production in proportion to its turnover than any other channels or platforms active in France. In return for the burden of these obligations, it has the right to broadcast the films it has helped to produce earlier. The succession of "windows" is as follows. First, the film must be released in theaters, then three or four months later, it is authorized for release on DVD or VoD, then third, between six and eight months after its first theatrical release, it can be released for the first time on pay channels, such as Canal+, if the channel has pre-financed the production of the film in accordance with its regulatory obligations. Then (fourth), between 15 and 17 months later, it can be released on a pay television channel that has not financed the film. Fifth, between 20 and 22 months later, it can be released for the first time on a so-called free channel (financed by advertising or public funds) if the channel has pre-financed the production of the film in accordance with its obligatory regulations. Sixth, between 28 and 30 months, the film can be released on a free channel that has not funded its production, and can also be released on a SvoD platform if it has funded the production of the film as part of its regulated obligations. Seventh, between 36 and 34 months, the film can be released on a platform that has not funded its production, and finally, eighth, after 42 or 44 months, the film can be released for free on any platform.
2 A large part of the expenditure that channels must devote to film or television production under their regulatory obligations must benefit so-called independent producers (that is to say, production companies that do not belong to television channels). This rule, which channels have been reluctant to accept, is being relaxed. The outlines of future obligations are not yet known at the time of writing, however.

3 The notion of control comes from financial economics and designates the link between the nature and the structure of the shareholding, on the one hand, and its management on the other hand. There are three main forms of control: First, control can be "public". In this situation, the company is owned by an individual under public law, who appoints the management board. Second, control can be "managerial". The shareholding is then very dispersed and no shareholder has enough shares to have a decisive influence on the management of the company. Managers succeed one another by co-optation and are relatively autonomous from the shareholders. Third, control can be family or personal: a person or a family (the Bolloré family in the case of Vivendi) owns enough shares in the company to be able to appoint the directors of the company and influence their decisions or even control management themselves.

References

AFP, "Financier habile, Vincent Bolloré a bâti un empire très diversifié", *DH Les Sports*, 26 April 2014. http://www.dhnet.be/dernieres-depeches/afp/financier-habile-vincent-bollore-a-bati-un-empire-tres-diversifie-53a999a83570c0e74341bd20

Beaufils, Vincent, "Comment Vincent Bolloré a préparé la succession de son empire", *Challenges*, 1 June 2019. https://www.challenges.fr/entreprise/comment-vincent-bollore-a-prepare-sa-succession_656905

Bolloré Group, "Rapport d'activité annuel", 2019. https://www.bollore.com/bollo-content/uploads/2020/05/boll_2002126_rapport_activite_2019_fr_mel_06-05-20.pdf

Bouquillion, Philippe, "La propriété étrangère dans les industries de la culture et de la communication en France", in "La propriété étrangère en radio diffusion: le débat canadien à la lumière de l'expérience étrangère", dir. Giroux Daniel, Sauvageau François, Tremblay Gaëtan. *Les Cahiers Médias*, no. 15, 2004, 63–92.

Bouquillion, Philippe, *Les industries de la culture et de la communication. Les stratégies du capitalisme.* Grenoble: Presses Universitaires de Grenoble, 2008.

Bouquillion, Philippe, "Cultural Diversity in the Country of Cultural Exception", in Luis A. Albornoz, M. Trinidad Garcia Leiva, *Audiovisual Industries and Diversity. Economics and Politics in the Digital Era*, London, New York: Routledge, 2019, 50–67.

Challenges Room Press, "The 500 largest fortunes in France", *Challenges*, 3 July 2020. https://www.challenges.fr/classements/fortune/vincent-bollore_85

Conseil Supérieur de l'Audiovisuel, "Deux années d'application de la réglementation de 2010 relative à la contribution des éditeurs de services de télévision au développement de la production télévisuelle", 13 January 2013. https://www.csa.fr/Informer/Collections-du-CSA/Thema-Toutesles-etudes-realisees-ou-co-realisees-par-le-CSA-sur-des-themes-specifiques/Les-etudes-du-CSA/Deux-annees-d-application-de-la-reglementation-de-2010-relative-a-la-contribution-des-editeurs-de-services-de-television-au-developpement-de-la-production-audiovisuelle

Dalloz Press Room, "Le plan Culture d'Emmanuel Macron passe par la transposition de la directive SMA", *Dalloz Actualités*, 13 May 2020. https://www.dalloz-actualite.fr/flash/plan-culture-d-emmanuel-macron-passe-par-transposition-de-directive-sma#.X4cBGVngr-Y

Hotelling, Harold, "Stability in Competition", *Economic Journal*, 1929, vol. 39, no. 1, p. 41.

La Tribune Press Room, "Succès de l'OPE sur Havas: le rêve de Bolloré prend forme", *La Tribune*, 15 January 2015. http://www.latribune.fr/technos-medias/medias/20150115tribb74216ef5/succes-de-l-ope-sur-havas-le-reve-de-bollore-prend-forme.html

Le Monde Press Room, "Bolloré se dit "honoré" d'accueillir M. Sarkozy, après Blum et Mohammed V", *Le Monde*, 20 June 2007. https://www.lemonde.fr/societe/article/2007/05/09/m-bollore-se-dit-honore-d-accueillir-m-sarkozy-apres-blum-et-mohammed-v_907684_3224.html

Miège, Bernard, "À l'arrière-plan des récents mouvements de concentration", *Les dossiers de l'audiovisuel*, 2000, no. 94, pp. 18–20.

Ministère de la Culture et de la Communication, "Chiffres clés 2020. Statistiques de la culture et de la communication", "Médias et industries culturelles", 2020, 32–32. https://www.culture.gouv.fr/Sites-thematiques/Etudes-et-statistiques/Publications2/Collections-d-ouvrages/Chiffres-cles-statistiques-de-la-culture-et-de-la-communication-2012-2020/Chiffres-cles-2020

Péan, Pierre and Nick Christophe, *TF1, un pouvoir*. Paris: Editions Fayard, 1997.

Piquard, Alexandre, "Canal+ dégaine son arme anti-Netflix", *Le Monde*, 12 March 2019. https://www.lemonde.fr/economie/article/2019/03/12/canal-degaine-son-arme-anti-netflix_5434795_3234.html.

Regourd, Serge, *L'exception culturelle*, Paris, Presses Universitaires de France, 2004.

Rousselot, Fabrice, "L'exception culturelle est morte", *Libération*, Paris, 18 December 2001. www.liberation.fr/evenement/2001/12/18/l-exception-culturelle-francaise-est-morte_387597

Steiner, Peter O., "Program Patterns and Preferences, The Workability of Competition in Radio Broadcasting", *Quarterly Journal of Economics*, vol. 66, no. 2, 194–223, 1952.

Tosseri, Olivier, "Bolloré quitte le pacte d'actionnaires de Mediobanca", *Les Echos*, 27 September 2018. https://www.lesechos.fr/finance-marches/banque-assurances/bollore-quitte-le-pacte-dactionnaires-de-mediobanca-140239

Vivendi, "Rapport d'activité annuel", 2019. https://www.vivendi.com/wp-content/uploads/2020/03/20200311-VIV_Vivendi-URD-2019.pdf

5 Vivendi's Cultural Profile

The aim of this chapter is to better identify Vivendi's main cultural characteristics and cultural issues raised by the company's strategies. These characteristics and challenges are the products of Vivendi's long history and are also closely linked to its economic and political profiles. Vivendi's cultural characteristics raise economic, financial and aesthetic issues, as well as questions related to public space.

Vivendi, a Company Mainly Active in the Cultural and Media Economy

Since the arrival of Vincent Bolloré at the head of Vivendi, the company's executives have emphasized its specialization in content:

> Since 2014, Vivendi has been working to build a world leader in culture, at the crossroads of entertainment, media and communication. [...] Being among the world leaders in media, content and communication means developing in several sectors. The group is thus present in music (UMG); television and cinema (Canal+ Group); communication (Havas Group); video games (Gameloft); digital platforms (Dailymotion); live shows and ticketing (Vivendi Village); and publishing, since the takeover of Editis in early 2019.
>
> (Vivendi, 2019: 15)

The company's financial communication emphasizes the strategic nature of its content. Entertainment is said to be Vivendi's DNA while its core business is "talent" management (see Chapter 2). Aside from its subsidiary the Havas Group and its stake in Telecom Italia, Vivendi's subsidiaries are mainly active in content. Vivendi's turnover is overwhelmingly generated from activities

Table 5.1 Breakdown of income by category

Types of income	2019 (in millions of euros)	2018 (in millions of euros)
Intellectual property licenses	8,042	6,508
Subscription services	4,599	4,474
Advertising, merchandising and others	3,322	3,008
Elimination of operations between company subsidiaries	−65	−58
Total turnover	15,898	13,932

Table created by the author (source: Vivendi, 2019: 248)

directly linked to the exploitation of content. As shown in Table 5.1, Vivendi's most significant income over the two years derives from intellectual property licenses, representing more than 50.5% of Vivendi's total turnover in 2019. The second source of income is comprised of subscription services. In the same year, these represented 28.9% of the company's turnover. Together, these two sources of revenue represent 79.5% of Vivendi's total revenue. The third source of income declared by the company is a very heterogeneous sum of "Advertising, merchandising and others." This includes income from cultural activities and especially advertising revenue from the commercial channels of the Canal+ Group, although the exact amount of this advertising revenue is not specified.

Within income directly derived from cultural content, that stemming from intellectual property licenses plays a particular role. Not only is this the most important source of income, but it is also the one demonstrating the highest growth, +23.57% between 2018 and 2019, while revenue from subscriptions only increased by +2.79%. Two observations can be made in this regard. First, it would appear that platformization covers very different areas. Although UMG and the Canal+ Group are two of the subsidiaries that face platformization, the industrial movements at work in each are actually very different. Being a major player in the music industry, UMG is experiencing a sharp increase in its turnover due to the dynamism of the streaming market and the balance of power that the leading firms have put in place against streaming platforms. On the other hand, the Canal+ Group is in a very different industrial position. Platformization leads to exacerbation of the competition suffered by the company and therefore to mediocre financial results. Second, Vivendi appears to represent a trend at work within the cultural industries; namely, as digital technology is deployed, cultural businesses tend to increasingly promote their content on professional markets ("Business to Business"), and less to end-consumer markets ("Business to Consumers"). In this regard, the requests these actors made in the 1990s and 2000s to strengthen the principles of intellectual property rights are now bearing fruit. The example of Vivendi shows that these strategies consisting in content players demanding a strengthening of intellectual property rights – in terms of principles as well as conditions for application – were not only and probably not specifically intended to penalize end-user acts of piracy, as was put forward in the 1990s and 2000s. The challenge was to position right holders with regard to distributors. Today, industrial players who mainly distribute their content on business-to-business markets, including to streaming platform operators, are in a more enviable situation than those who, like the Canal+ Group, sell content directly to end-consumers.

Aesthetic Issues Linked to Specific Socio-Economic Models

Cultural issues are also aesthetic. Since the early 2000s, Vivendi has promoted a culture based primarily on industrial cultural products especially from the major US players. This commercial culture is associated with the promotion of globalization driven by large transnational actors like Vivendi Universal, which differs significantly from the strategy that led the company to its diversification in the media during the 1990s. The earlier approach was based on the hope that industrial players linked to the state, especially through public procurement, would promote French culture abroad and bolster France's cultural industries, contributing significantly to its GDP and employment rate. These hopes have been dashed, however. Today, Vivendi's contributions to public debates are mainly related to the defense of intellectual property rights (IPR), and therefore a willingness to promote artistic talents, including singers, musicians, actors and directors.

However, the varying cultural content offered by Vivendi presents significant aesthetic and economic differences. The socio-economic models at work within the various subsidiaries notably differ, with UMG and Editis corresponding to what theorists of cultural industries have called the "editorial" model (Miège, Pajon,

Salaün, 1986). Each of these groups includes many different firms, "labels" in the case of recorded music, and publishing houses in the case of book publishing. These entities can target very different segments, more or less mainstream and intended for a large audience or, conversely, intended for a small segment of the population. In addition, under the editorial model, the production costs of content are only partially assuming by "publishers" (of music or books). External producers or creators in recorded music, and authors in book publishing, can take on a significant share of the costs. The industrial players who mainly act as distributors in this specific case can therefore put a large number of titles on the market and assume the risk that some of these musical titles or books only reach a small audience. This same trend can also be observed in recorded music in many countries, with artists becoming producers. They retain their rights to the recordings and only entrust the major players in recorded music such as UMG with distribution tasks. Thus the major firms are able to negotiate distribution rights for an even larger number of titles without contributing to their production. In contrast, pay television services correspond more to the "club" model (Tremblay & Lacroix, 1991; Moeglin, 2007), under which the content broadcaster must assume a significant share of the production costs of original and exclusive content. What is more, platform development costs are also high. Operators are thus encouraged to mainly target the general public with mainstream content. Only some of the content may target smaller segments when production costs are low and it is broadcast on thematic satellite channels or via SVoD platforms.

Cultural Dimension and Attempts to Influence the Political Public Space

The issue surrounding Vivendi's strategies with regard to public space can be approached in two ways. On the one hand, through its financial communication, the company attempts to build a very positive image of its influence on the political or cultural public space, and on the other hand, beyond this discourse constructed by the company, it is the target of much criticism.

Building the Image of a Corporate Citizen in Vivendi's Financial Communications

Vivendi's financial communication emphasizes various dimensions of the company's activity considered to be positive for the public space or for society, such as the notion of sustainable development. For example "in 2019, 17% of the electricity used by the group was generated by renewable energy sources" (Vivendi, 2019: 54). Even more emphasis is placed on promoting diversity, in the various senses of the term. First, Vivendi's commitment to promoting women is clearly stated, both in terms of employment and the image of women and the company's content and advertising:

> Like Havas, the Canal+ Group strives to give a fair and balanced representation of the image of women through documentaries, films, series and advertising campaigns. [...] In 2019, 20% of films financed by Canal+ and 29% of films financed by Studiocanal were the work of female directors.
> (Vivendi, 2019: 59)

The company has set up various committees to this end:

> UMPG co-founded She Is The Music (SITM), a non-profit organization created to promote equality, inclusion and access to opportunities for women in the creative professions [...] Employees from UMPG and UMG have helped develop SITM, from creating its business plan and media properties to leading its three flagship initiatives: All-female songwriting camps around the world (hosted by renowned artists like Alicia Keys, Mary J. Blige, Tori Kelly, Anitta, Kim Petras and many more); developing the world's first and largest database of women in the music industry; and a major mentoring program to support the next generation of women in the industry, particularly in disadvantaged communities.
> (Vivendi, 2019: 60)

Furthermore, "the Canal+ Group set up a Diversity Committee in 2015. This committee, led by the head of diversity at the Canal+ and Vivendi groups, is notably responsible for ensuring balanced representation and not stereotypical diversity within the group's branches" (Vivendi, 2019: 60). Second, Vivendi is committed to promoting thematic diversity in content produced and distributed by the company. Entities of the company endeavor to address issues such as social violence. For example, the documentary Crime + Punishment dealt with police violence in the United States, as well as racism in football. In the same way, "the Canal+ Group has launched Hello on myCanal, a digital channel that offers the best of European and international LGBTQ + creations" (Vivendi, 2019: 59).

Likewise, the company has stated its aim to "give a fair place to people with disabilities [...] In 2019, the Canal+ Group channels devoted 35 reports to the issue of disability" (Vivendi, 2019: 60). Third, an emphasis is placed on youth and the "local" dimension.

> Local artists account for 61% of the company's revenue, underscoring its continued commitment to investing in local talent, infrastructure and skills [...] The company signs artists in nearly 60 countries, the albums recorded represent 44 languages and are available in 120 countries.
>
> (Vivendi, 2019: 58)

The company communication also notes the attention paid to African languages.

> The programs produced by Canal+ International are available in French for the most part, with possible inclusion, in series in particular, of vernacular languages (we can cite Wolof in Sakho & Mangane or Lingala in L'Amour à 200 meters) with subtitles in French. In 2019, Canal+ launched two channels in two other languages: all the programs are in Wolof on Sunu Yeuf and the same is true of Novegasy, which is in Malagasy.
>
> (Vivendi, 2019: 58)

Fourth, the company also highlights its commitment to information pluralism.

> Since 2008, an Ethics Charter has reiterated respect for the principles of information ethics. An Ethics Committee relating to the honesty, independence and pluralism of information and programs, made up of independent figures (under independence criteria established by law), has been set up at the level of the group by appointment of its members by the Canal+ Group supervisory board in September 2017. The Committee was not consulted during 2019. A Code of Ethics, jointly drafted and signed by management and representatives of journalists, specifies the ethical rules necessary for the preparation of independent, reliable, credible and rigorous information.
>
> (Vivendi, 2019: 60)

Vivendi's financial communication therefore builds the image of a citizen-oriented and modern company committed to the good causes of its times and whose objective cannot be reduced to a simple quest for profitability. These various commitments are not exclusive of other attempts to influence the public space, however. According to the various detractors of the company's management, numerous attempts have been made to control management of the company over editorial lines. Far from the image of a modern company open to diversity that is built into its financial communication, the practices of Vivendi's management and its direct interventions are reminiscent of the traditions of the more traditional media capitalism, where the owner of the company dictates the law and controls how teams work, especially journalists and television hosts.

The Many Controversies Surrounding Interventionism by Vivendi's Management

There is a vast literature, particularly in the political economy of communication, on the challenges of financialization and concentration for the political public space. Authors such as Herbert Schiller (1969) have questioned the issues of standardization of content and their inclusion with the aim of creating a political order. Contrarily, other authors outside of the critical sphere have sought to show that concentration has its advantages in terms of cultural diversity. These authors can refer to the model posited by Peter Steiner (1952). This question has been much debated in France, Vivendi's base, also by researchers in the political economy of communication. Authors who worked in the 1990s and 2000s have generally put forward the fact that attempts to control content and expression do not tend to only occur among the very large financialized players. These attempts at control are therefore mainly linked to the development of management control systems within the cultural and media industries (Robin, 2003). For example, small book publishers that are subject to strong profitability requirements by their management or shareholders develop such management controls – and therefore content control – more often than large publishers do. In addition, these controls are less political than financial. Content can be controlled or even formatted to correspond to the keys to success rather than to censor certain expressions or promote others. Research carried out in the 1990s and 2000s on the strategies of the main North American and European players in the cultural industries, then in a phase of high concentration and financialization, showed that the leaders of these large groups and even more the large players in the financial sphere that supported them were more sensitive to the evolution of overall profitability and the prospects for speculation of these industrial players than in a desire to control and censor content (Miège, 2000; Bouquillion, 2005). Above all, this research showed that the type of control employed (Pradié, 2003) influenced the propensity of company management to influence content for political reasons. Thus, so-called "managerial control" (the company has a fairly fragmented shareholding structure and control is exercised by a manager who does not own the company) generally leads to less political control than a situation of "family control" (a family or person owns enough shares to control the company). Vivendi Universal was under a regime of managerial control in the 1990s and 2000s, particularly when Jean-Marie Messier headed the company. However, since 2015 and the takeover by Vincent Bolloré and his family group, Vivendi has been in a situation of family and even personal control. Despite that, numerous recent attempts at political control or direct influence over the content and even censorship have been reported in the press.

Many such cases are found in the Canal+ Group's French and African subsidiaries. According to accusations in the press, Vincent Bolloré has personally decided to fire many people, including managers but also star presenters and well-known journalists, while he has imposed his own replacements. For example, a comedian, Sébastien Thoen, was fired at the end of 2020 after he caricatured a program called "L'heure des Pros" on Canal+. "L'heure des Pros" is a flagship program of the permanent news channel Cnews, belonging to the Canal+ Group. Headed by Pascal Praud, the show breaks audience records each morning. According to the newspaper *Le Parisien,* it was not Pascal Praud who asked for his dismissal, but Vincent Bolloré himself: "Some within the channel's management tried to oppose it, but they could do nothing against the will of the big boss. 'This is the act of the prince', said an employee who attended the entire process" (Daragon et al., 2020). Thoen had worked at Canal+ for 17 years. Then, a Canal+ sports journalist, Stéphane Guy, was fired at the end of December 2020 for expressing his support for Sébastien Thoen. He himself had worked at the station for 20 years.[1] The program in question, which presents very reactionary points of view, is very representative of the type of programs and the climate that Vincent Bolloré established after his arrival at the head of Vivendi and therefore of the Canal+ Group. The editorial line adopted by Canal+ is highly politicized. Figures belonging to the very conservative right or even the extreme right are frequently invited to broadcasts or even host programs.

Stéphane Guy's dismissal reveals a more general type of relationship that Vincent Bolloré has established with Canal+ employees and especially journalists. In 2016, when Canal+ journalists had been on strike for more than a month to protest the new directives issued by Vincent Bolloré and his decision to install a controversial figure, Jean-Marc Morandini, as presentator of news programmes, Pascal Praud had been accused of taking the side of the channel's management against the striking journalists (Vigneau, 2018). He then explained himself by declaring:

> When I was at TF1, I was 100% TF1. When I was at Football Club Nantes, I was 100% FC Nantes. And today, at CNEWS, I am 100% Bolloré. [...] If we are not happy, we leave, we do not spit in the soup. Loyalty is a value that I place above everything because I hate traitors.[2]

These comments were very badly received by French journalists, due to the tradition of journalists' independence from media owners in France. Guaranteed by law, it is an essential characteristic of the work of a journalist and what distinguishes them from communicators.

In addition, programs are thought to have been deleted, modified or created at Bolloré's personal behest. For example, a satirical program called "Les Guignols de l'Info" was deleted in 2018, having been broadcast since 1988. This program, which Bolloré had already wanted to scrap back in 2015, was extremely popular, caricaturing French celebrities and especially politicians. All the important personalities of the day had their own puppets. For example, President François Mitterrand was represented in the form of a frog. Rightly or wrongly, this program was deemed to have a major influence on politicians' popularity. It is true that audience ratings had dropped at the time the show was axed, but it is also true that politicians hated it. We have already noted the links between Vincent Bolloré and French political circles, and it is therefore difficult not to see a link between the desire to maintain close relations with the said circles and the suppression of this show. Likewise, in 2017, "Le Grand Journal", Canal+'s flagship political program, which very often took a critical or even acerbic tone toward politicians, was canceled. Again, the reasons given were poor ratings. However, Vincent Bolloré has never hidden his hostility toward mockery and a certain freedom of tone that characterized

Canal+ from its creation until the takeover by the Bolloré Group. In 2015, he declared on public radio France Inter that he thought Canal+ was sometimes

> a little too derisory. I prefer it when they are more about discovery than derision. Because sometimes it's a little hurtful or unpleasant [...] I find that making fun of yourself is good. Making fun of others is less so.³

One-off cases of censorship have also been mentioned in the press. For example, in May 2015, according to the major political newspaper, Le Monde, and the online news magazine Mediapart, Vincent Bolloré is said to have personally intervened to prevent the broadcast of an investigative documentary dedicated to a French bank, Crédit Mutuel, Canal+.

> In mid-May, Vivendi's largest shareholder [...] telephoned the CEO of Canal+, Rodolphe Belmer (since sacked) and invoked his links with Michel Lucas, the boss of Crédit Mutuel [...] In the report [...], the bank is accused of promoting tax evasion practices among its customers.
>
> (Piquard, 2015)

Likewise, censorship cases can be linked to Bolloré's activities in Africa. Thus, in 2017, an NGO defending journalists and press freedom, Reporters Without Borders, alerted the media and the Canal+ ethics committee after a documentary was withdrawn from the Canal+ Group platforms for several days, before subsequently reappearing. In addition, two employees were fired, a programming manager and the director of channels and content for Canal+ International, François Deplanck. The documentary, which lasted about ten minutes, showed demonstrations against the President of Togo, Faure Gnassingbé. However, it was broadcast just before Vincent Bolloré's visit to the country. Togo is one of the privileged partners of the Bolloré Group in Africa, the company notably operating the Lomé container port there. Vivendi has also opened a cinema complex in Togo, CanalOlympia (Sénéjoux, 2017).

In addition to accusations of censorship, Vivendi's media are also said to widely practice self-promotion or the promotion of the Bolloré Group's activities in Africa. A well-known French weekly, L'Express, carried out an investigation into this subject.

> 'There is a violation of Canal+' editorial line', wrote journalist Jean-Baptiste Rivoire, editor-in-chief [...] and member of the Society of Canal Journalists. 'Vincent Bolloré is turning Canal+ into a banana republic.' [...] One Canal+ journalist interviewed by L'Express comments that the pressure to broadcast images of self-promotion in favor of Bolloré is 'almost constant'.
>
> (Kucinskas, 2018)

Equally, a documentary on public television devoted to Vincent Bolloré's activities in Africa has claimed that when "Bolloré inaugurates a performance hall, for example in Guinea, he asks the teams to report on it" (ibid.). Likewise, the newspaper Direct Matin, belonging to Bolloré, was previously presented as systematically promoting the free-to-use electric car service offered by the Bolloré Group, Autolib. In addition, "Direct Matin also offers monthly subscriptions to Autolib as prizes for its promotional contests" (Pelletier, 2016). To sum up, Bolloré's interventions lead to a blurring of the line between information and advertising.

Vincent Bolloré has acquired a reputation for his brutal treatment of journalists, which can harm him when attempting to implement his strategies. For instance, at the end of 2020, at a time when Bernard Arnault and Vincent Bolloré were in competition to influence the management of the Lagardère group, the former achieved some success purely because Bolloré is so feared, placing one of his allies, the director of external relations at LVMH, Jean-Charles Tréhan, within Lagardère. "While Vincent Bolloré's brutality with journalists makes people talk, the influence games played by the director of external relations at LVMH [Jean-Charles Tréhan], who now also watches over Lagardère's media, remain quiet enough so as not to attract attention" (Chemin, 2020).

Conclusion

Now we have reached the end of this book, some answers can be given to the three questions that arise around Vivendi and other global media giants.

What Is "Global" about an Industrial Player such as Vivendi?

Observation of the Vivendi case reveals the difficulty of characterizing the transnational dimension of such a company. The first question relates to the importance of foreign markets in Vivendi's financial results. Although the geographical distribution of financial results provides us with an overview, the aggregated data may hide very heterogeneous realities. Numerical indicators can be misleading. Beyond the quantitative aspects, we must consider how transnationalization contributes to the economic dynamism of the activities considered. This contribution is fundamental in the case of UMG, as music titles can be sold on an almost global scale, excluding areas where informal economy is widespread or those where the propensity to pay is low. On the other hand, in the case of the Canal+ Group, transnationalization results more from a juxtaposition of national positions, the transnational circulation of audiovisual and cinematographic works produced by the Canal+ Group being lower. A second question derives from the first. Does a transnationalized company such as Vivendi promote a transnational culture or, contrarily, favor the defense of national identities? We have observed that when possible, and especially when content is easily transnationalized, the company's interest is to offer the same, most attractive content in different territories, even to the detriment of national content. The French example shows the extent to which promoting national content is mainly the result of a public policy, the rule of "cultural exception", which, despite its reluctance, the company is forced to apply. Finally, the transnationalization of a company such as Vivendi must also be analyzed from the point of view of the complex games of political and economic influence it engages in at the transnational scale. Vivendi's activity is notably linked to the challenges facing the Bolloré Group, especially in Africa. Although Vivendi may benefit from this activity, it must avoid harming the African interests of the Bolloré Group.

How Does Inclusion in a Company such as Vivendi Weigh on the Activities of the Cultural and Media Industries Brought Together under It?

The question arises insofar as Vivendi is a financialized, transnationalized company that operates in concentrated markets. A study of the Vivendi case confirms the need to clearly distinguish between what is playing out at the level of the holding company from that which is playing out at the level of each of the subsidiaries, or even sub-components, while also understanding the interrelationships between the two levels. The purpose of the holding company is to generate financial value, and especially dividends, for shareholders, because Vivendi is not positioned in high growth markets such as those more directly linked to the digital sphere. Given this, it is vital that the subsidiaries generate the highest possible EBITA. On the other hand, being part of this conglomerate holding company is of only limited importance for the subsidiaries and their sub-components, as the synergies between the various subsidiaries are very low. These subsidiaries and sub-components can benefit from financial contributions to evolve, especially when their EBITA is low or negative. This is particularly the case with the activities grouped together under Vivendi Village, although these are only of marginal economic importance within Vivendi for the time being, their interest being more symbolic. By way of example, L'Olympia is a legendary performance hall in Paris, and holding promotional events there is appealing for the company. Integration into the holding company means that subsidiaries achieving a positive EBITA see a significant portion of their results not invested for the benefit of their future industrial development but distributed in the form of dividends by the holding company or contributing to the share buyback program. They are cash cows for the holding company. In this respect, financialization does not provide additional resources to the subsidiaries, but rather it is the wealth created by the subsidiaries that feeds the players interested in the financialization of Vivendi and first and foremost the Bolloré Group.

Is the Existence of a Large Financialized Corporation like Vivendi a Threat to Democracy?

The direct intervention of the company directors in the editorial line is blatant and disregards ethical tradition. This is not linked to financialization, but rather the result of the personal power wielded by the chief shareholder and leader of the company. The importance of family control in the cultural and media industries in France, and especially within Vivendi, the largest French industrial player in this sector, constitutes a proven threat to information pluralism. Controlling an industrial player like Vivendi also allows an individual to be a powerful player in the games of influence in political and economic circles, the two being very intertwined in France, a country where the state intervenes in the economy in many ways, including in the cultural and media industries.

Notes

1 Clérat, Antoine, *Foot 365*, 18 December 2020. https://www.football365.fr/cest-fin-stephane-guy-canal-9941057.html#item=1

2 Source: Jeanmarcmorandini.com, 18 November 2017, https://www.jeanmarcmorandini.com/article-374813-pascal-praud-je-suis-100-bollore-si-on-n-est-pas-content-on-part-on-ne-crache-pas-dans-la-soupe-je-hais-les-traitres.html?fbclid=IwAR0JjsG6b44C5yvcIDFcud_MEgDkxntW0SbhyCNwfkkR3BJyOeCDp5qap-0

3 Source: Meffre, Benjamin, *Pure médias*, 12 February 2015. https://www.ozap.com/actu/vincent-bollore-sur-l-esprit-canal-c-est-parfois-un-peu-trop-de-derision/462667

References

Bouquillion, Philippe, "La constitution des pôles des industries de la culture de la communication. Entre coups financiers et intégration de filières industrielles", *Réseaux*, 131, 111–144, 2005.

Chemin, Ariane, "L'un des hommes de confiance de Bernard Arnault place des fidèles dans les médias de LVMH et Lagardère", *Le Monde*, 21 December 2020. https://www.lemonde.fr/economie/article/2020/12/21/l-un-des-hommes-de-confiance-de-bernard-arnault-place-des-fideles-dans-les-medias-de-lvmh-et-lagardere_6064095_3234.html

Daragon, Benoît, Merle Sylvain and Zoltobroda Michaël, "Sébastien Thoen viré de Canal+ après sa parodie de Pascal Praud", *Le Parisien*, 27 November 2020. https://www.leparisien.fr/culture-loisirs/tv/sebastien-thoen-vire-de-canal-apres-sa-parodie-de-pascal-praud-27-11-2020-8410899.php

Kucinskas, Audrey, "Autopromo, censure: Bolloré fait-il de Canal+ 'une république bananière'"? *L'Express*, 18 January 2018. https://www.lexpress.fr/actualite/medias/autopromo-censure-bollore-fait-il-de-canal-une-republique-bananiere_1977233.html

Miège, Bernard, "À l'arrière-plan des récents mouvements de concentration", *Les dossiers de l'audiovisuel*, no. 94, 18–20, 2000.

Miège, Bernard, Patrick Pajon and Jean-Michel Salaün, *L'industrialisation de l'audiovisuel. Des programmes pour de nouveaux médias*. Grenoble: Presses Universitaires de Grenoble, 1986.

Mœglin, Pierre, "Des modèles socio-économiques en mutation", in Philippe Bouquillion and Yolande Combès (dir.), *Les industries de la culture et de la communication en mutation*. Paris: L'Harmattan, 2007, 151–162.

Pelletier, Nicolas, "Direct matin ne se lasse pas de ses scoops sur Autolib", *L'Obs & Rue 89*, 18 November 2016. https://www.nouvelobs.com/rue89/rue89-medias/20130624.RUE7227/direct-matin-ne-se-lasse-pas-de-ses-scoops-sur-autolib.html

Piquard, Alexandre, "Canal+: Bolloré accusé d'avoir censuré un documentaire", *Le Monde*, 29 July 2015. https://www.lemonde.fr/economie/article/2015/07/29/canal-bollore-accuse-d-avoir-censure-un-documentaire-sur-le-credit-mutuel_4703807_3234.html

Pradié, Christian, "Comment penser la question de la détention et du contrôle des industries de la culture et de la communication", in Bernard

Miège and Gaëtan Tremblay (dir.), *2001 Bogues, Globalisme et pluralisme*. Québec: Presses de l'Université Laval, 2003, 405–419.

Robin, Christian, "La gestion et le contenu des livres", *Les enjeux de l'information et la communication*, no. 04/1, 2003. https://lesenjeux.univ-grenoble-alpes.fr/2003/varia/08-la-gestion-et-le-contenu-des-livres

Schiller, Herbert, *Mass Communication and American Empire*. Boston, MA: Beacon Press, 1969.

Sénéjoux, Richard, "Censure sur Canal+: Vincent Bolloré dans le viseur de Reporters sans frontières", *Télérama*, 20 December 2017. https://www.telerama.fr/medias/vincent-bollore-dans-le-viseur-de-reporter-sans-frontieres, n5409042.php

Steiner, Peter O., "Program Patterns and Preferences, The Workability of Competition in Radio Broadcasting", *Quarterly Journal of Economics*, vol. 66, no. 2, 194–223, 1952.

Tremblay, Gaëtan and Jean-Guy Lacroix, *Télévision Deuxième Dynastie*. Québec: Presses de l'Université. du Québec, 1991.

Vigneau, Nathalie, "Nathalie, Pascal Praud "taupe" de Vincent Bolloré pendant les grèves à iTélé?", *TéléStar*, 2 March 2018. https://www.telestar.fr/actu-tv/autres-emissions/pascal-praud-taupe-de-vincent-bollore-pendant-les-greves-a-itele-decouvrez-sa-reaction-333340

Vivendi, "Rapport d'activité annuel", 2019. https://www.vivendi.com/wp-content/uploads/2020/03/20200311-VIV_Vivendi-URD-2019.pdf

Index

Activision 19, 20, 21, 24, 25
Activision Blizzard 32, 67
advertising 1, 2, 4, 9, 10, 11, 17, 29, 31, 36, 40, 48, 55, 56, 60, 61, 64, 75, 78, 80, 84, 85, 89, 95, 99, 102, 108
Africa 1, 3, 41, 44, 45, 53, 62, 93, 107, 108, 109
African 1, 103, 105, 109
Alphabet 2
Amazon 2, 50, 59, 68
Amber (Amber Capital) 37, 38, 39, 71
American 3, 7, 8, 15, 18, 23, 24, 33, 44, 49, 50, 56, 67, 75, 81, 82, 83, 84, 88, 89, 91, 104, 112
AMF (Autorité des Marchés Financiers) 31, 69
Apple 1, 46, 59, 60, 61, 68
Arnault, Bernard 37, 38, 39, 40, 65, 69, 71, 108, 111
Asia 3, 44, 45
Asian 36, 44
AT&T 2
artificial intelligence 44
audiovisual 1, 2, 3, 4, 10, 12, 14, 15, 19, 20, 23, 28, 29, 30, 43, 47, 49, 50, 58, 74, 75, 77, 78, 79, 80, 81, 82, 83, 84, 85, 86, 87, 88, 94, 109
AVMS (Audiovisual Media Services) 86
AXA 18

Banijay(Group Holding) 1, 28, 40, 41, 70
bankruptcy 1, 17, 18, 21, 23, 38
BeIN Sports 49, 52

Bébéar (Jean-Claude) 18
Berlusconi 1, 3, 18, 29, 30
Bertelsmann 2, 7, 22
Blizzard 19, 20
blockchain 44
BMG 20
Bolloré Group 5, 6, 20, 22, 28, 31, 65, 67, 89, 90, 92, 93, 94, 96, 107, 108, 109, 110
Bolloré, Vincent 5, 21, 22, 23, 24, 25, 28, 31, 37, 38, 39, 40, 43, 67, 73, 89, 91, 92, 93, 93, 96, 98, 105, 106, 107, 108, 111, 112
Bolloré, Yannick 31, 43, 44, 56, 89, 91, 92
book (book publishing and book industry) 1, 2, 3, 4, 9, 10, 11, 12, 19, 32, 36, 37, 39, 40, 43, 56, 57, 58, 98 101, 104
Brazil 2, 16, 19, 20
Brazilian 19, 22
broadcasting 17, 49, 52, 76, 81, 97, 112
broadcasting rights 29, 49, 52, 75, 76, 79, 80
BskyB 14, 15
bubble (internet bubble, financial bubble) 1, 4, 17

Canal+ 1, 2, 9, 10, 11, 14, 15, 16, 17, 19, 20, 21, 22, 23, 29, 41, 42, 43, 45, 47, 48, 49, 50, 51, 52, 53, 54, 55, 63, 64, 65, 68, 69, 70, 71, 75, 76, 77 78, 79, 80, 81, 82, 84, 86, 87, 88, 89, 95, 97, 98, 99, 100, 102, 103, 105, 106, 107, 108, 109, 111, 112

Index

Canal Play 51
cable (cable-TV, cable networks, cable operator) 4, 10, 11, 12, 15, 16, 18, 23
Caisse des Dépôtset Consignations 90
Canal Satellite 14, 15
capitalism 1, 2, 8, 12, 18, 36, 89, 91, 92, 93, 104
Cegetel 11, 19, 20
censorship 79, 105, 107
CGE (Compagnie Générale des Eaux) 8, 9, 10, 11, 12, 13, 14, 17
China 41, 44, 59
Chinese 2, 3, 36, 49
cinema 14, 15, 20, 41, 47, 48, 54, 76, 77, 78, 79, 80, 81, 82, 84, 85, 88, 98, 107
CNC (Center for Cinema and Animated Image) 80, 81
concentration 1, 7, 97, 104, 111
competition 50, 51, 52, 63, 73, 74, 75, 76, 81, 83, 84, 85, 86, 88, 97, 100, 108, 112
conglomerate 4, 17, 20, 40, 63, 110
convergence 4, 10, 12, 20, 56
Conseil Supérieur de l'Audiovisuel 85, 89, 96
cross-ownership 74
cultural exception 3, 4, 73, 76, 77, 81, 82, 83, 84, 96, 109
cultural diversity 82, 83, 96, 104

Dailymotion 1, 28, 98
debt(s) 5, 18, 23, 25, 28, 32, 34, 38
digital 1, 3, 4, 36, 50, 54, 59, 61, 63, 74, 76, 84, 85, 96, 98, 100, 102, 110
Direct 8 22
Direct Star 22, 75, 89
Discovery 50, 107
Disney 2, 28, 52, 53, 59, 60, 87
dividend(s) 27, 37, 40, 63, 64, 65, 66, 67, 68, 89, 90, 109, 110
DMCA (Digital Millennium Copyright Act) 74

Echo Star 19
Editis 1, 10, 32, 38, 40, 41, 42, 43, 45, 56, 57, 58, 69, 72, 98, 100

Elliott 33, 34, 65, 70, 71, 72
EMI 20
ESPN 17
Endemol 28, 70
Etisalat 24
Europe 1, 2, 3, 16, 18, 19, 44, 53, 81, 82
European 10, 11, 14, 15, 28, 29, 30, 45, 62, 65, 68, 74, 80, 86, 87, 88, 93, 102, 104
Eurosport 17, 53

film(s) 11, 14, 19, 29, 46, 47, 48, 49, 52, 54, 55, 58, 75, 76, 77, 79, 80, 81, 84, 86, 87, 88, 95, 102
FNAC 35, 64, 70
financialization 1, 6, 27, 84, 92, 104, 110
Fininvest 29, 30
Fourtou (Jean-René) 18, 21, 22, 23
France Telecom 19
free 9, 20, 33, 47, 48, 52, 60, 61, 75, 82, 83, 90, 95, 108

game(s) 1, 4, 14, 17, 19, 20, 21, 24, 27, 28, 31, 32, 39, 40, 46, 52, 56, 58, 59, 60, 61, 66, 67, 83, 98, 108, 109, 110
Gameloft 1, 31, 32, 40, 41, 42, 59, 60, 61, 63, 66, 70, 98
General Electric 19
globalization 64, 82, 84, 100
Google 55, 59, 68
Granada 15
Guillemot (Family) 32, 70
GVT (Global Village Telecom) 19, 20, 21, 22, 23, 24, 25, 67

Hachette 2, 11, 32, 37, 38, 64
HADOPI (High Authority for the Dissemination of works and Protection of rights on the Internet) 74
Havas 1, 9, 10, 11, 13, 31, 40, 41, 42, 43, 45, 55, 56, 64, 69, 71, 78, 89, 97, 98, 102
HBO 50, 53, 71, 79
horizontal diversification 4, 12, 14
Houghton Mifflin 19

ICT 2, 4, 19
Iliad 33, 52, 69
IPR (Intellectual Property Rights) 58, 73, 74, 100
international 9, 14, 17, 19, 31, 38, 39, 41, 44, 47, 48, 53, 54, 56, 59, 60; 91, 93, 102, 103, 107
Internet 1, 4, 15, 18, 19, 22, 33, 34, 46, 48, 52, 70, 74
Italy: I, 3, 19, 29, 30, 35, 39, 93
Italian 24, 29, 30, 33, 34, 64, 74, 93

Lagardère 2, 5, 16, 32, 36, 37, 38, 39, 40, 64, 65, 69, 71, 108, 111
Lévy (Jean-Bernard) 18, 19, 21, 25
live 1, 4, 14, 41, 43, 47, 61, 62, 98
LVMH 38, 108, 111

M6 2, 76, 80, 87
M7 53, 54, 64, 68, 69
Madrigall 32
Maroc Telecom 16, 20, 21, 24, 25, 67
Mediaset 1, 3, 29, 30, 40, 41, 65, 69, 71, 93
merchandising 41, 43, 46, 47, 99
merger 4, 11, 14, 15, 20, 35, 75, 76
Messier (Jean-Marie) 13, 14, 15, 16, 18, 19, 23, 82, 83, 88, 92, 105
Microsoft 59, 68
Morocco 3, 16, 19, 94
MultiThématiques 16
Murdoch 15
music 1, 2, 3, 4, 14, 15, 17, 20, 21, 23, 28, 35, 36, 40, 41, 43, 44, 45, 46, 47, 56, 58, 69, 70, 73, 74, 94, 98, 99, 101, 102, 109

NBCUniversal 50
Netflix 2, 3, 10, 23, 29, 30, 49, 50, 51, 52, 70, 71, 86, 87, 97
Netherlands 30, 53, 86
Newscorp 17
Numericable 11, 17, 23

Orange 19, 20, 28, 50, 52, 71, 76, 85, 87

Pathé 14
Pearson 15

Planeta 32, 72
platform(s) 1, 3, 4, 28, 30, 46, 49, 50, 53, 54, 59, 60, 61, 63, 73, 76, 81, 84, 85, 86, 87, 88, 95, 98, 99, 100, 101, 107
platformization 63, 68, 99, 100
pluralism 30, 103, 110
Poland 16
policy 4, 6, 14, 21, 39, 51, 52, 57, 73, 74, 76, 77, 78, 79, 81, 88, 109
Puyfontaine (Arnaud de) 23, 56, 58, 92

quota(s) 76, 80, 84, 86

regulation(s) 6, 74, 79, 80, 81, 84, 85, 86, 87, 88, 95
regulatory 6, 33, 73, 77, 80, 82, 84, 85, 87, 89, 95
Richemont 16
RTL 2

Sarkozy (Nicolas) 38, 93, 97
SFR 11, 19, 20, 21, 22, 23, 50, 60, 67
Seagram 15
Seydoux (Jérôme) 14
SoftBank 17
Sony 2, 7, 15, 74
Spain 30
Spanish 29, 30, 32, 49
Spotify 63
subscription(s) 15, 46, 48, 49, 51, 52, 60, 61, 78, 84, 99, 108
streaming 4, 46, 47, 52, 63, 73, 99, 100
StudioCanal 11, 29, 41, 48, 54, 75, 102
SVoD (Subscription Video on Demand) 49, 50, 51, 52, 76, 81, 84, 86, 88, 95, 101
synergies 4, 5, 12, 16, 18, 21, 22, 24, 26, 27, 40, 43, 45, 47, 54, 56, 58, 63, 64, 66, 68, 110

Telecom Italia 1, 3, 24, 30, 33, 34, 35, 40, 41, 65, 68, 69, 70, 71, 72, 93, 98
telecommunications 3, 4, 10, 11, 12, 16, 17, 18, 19, 20, 21, 22, 24,

25, 28, 33, 40, 50, 52, 59, 67, 68, 75, 85
Telefonica 23, 24, 25
Telephony 11, 15, 16, 22
Telepiu 19
Tencent 2, 7, 35, 36, 69, 70
theaters 14, 43, 61, 62, 81, 95
TF1 2, 17, 20, 21, 76, 79, 80, 87, 94, 97, 106
Time Warner 2, 15
TPS 20, 53, 75

Ubisoft 31, 32, 70
UMG (Universal Music Group) 1, 2, 20, 23, 35, 36, 37, 40, 41, 42, 43, 45, 46, 47, 63, 65, 69, 74, 98, 99, 100, 101, 102, 109
United Kingdom 14, 62
United States 1, 10, 12, 14, 15, 16, 19, 41, 62, 74, 81, 88, 102

Universal Studios 15
USA Networks 15, 82

Veolia 17, 62
vertical integration 4, 12, 15, 51
Vivendi Environment 17
VUE (Vivendi Universal Entertainment) 19, 82
Vivendi Universal 2, 3, 4, 11, 12, 15, 16, 17, 18, 19, 20, 25, 32, 40, 81, 82, 88, 92, 100, 105
VUP (Vivendi Universal Publishing) 11, 32
Vivendi Village: VI, 1, 40, 41, 42, 61, 63, 66, 98, 110
Vodafone 15

Wendel 32
WTO (World Trade Organization) 84